	DATE DUE		

Studies in
Writing & Rhetoric

IN 1980, THE CONFERENCE ON COLLEGE COMPOSITION AND COM-
munication perceived a need for providing publishing opportunities for monographs that were too lengthy for publication in its
journal and too short for the typical publication of scholarly books
by The National Council of Teachers of English. A series called
Studies in Writing and Rhetoric was conceived, and a Publication
Committee established.

Monographs to be considered by publication may be specula-
tive, theoretical, historical, or analytical studies; research reports;
or other works contributing to a better understanding of writing,
including interdisciplinary studies or studies in disciplines related
to composing. The SWR series will exclude textbooks, unrevised
dissertations, book-length manuscripts, course syllabi, lesson plans,
and collections of previously published material.

Any teacher-writer interested in submitting a work for publication in this series should send either a prospectus and sample
manuscript or a full manuscript to the NCTE Director of Publications, 1111 Kenyon Road, Urbana, IL 61801. Accompanied by
sample manuscript, a prospectus should contain a rationale, a definition of readership within the CCCC constituency, comparison
with related publications, an annotated table of contents, an esti-
mate of length in double-spaced 8½ × 11 sheets, and the date by
which full manuscript can be expected. Manuscripts should be in
the range of 100 to 170 typed manuscript pages.

The works that have been published in this series serve as models
for future SWR monographs.

Paul O'Dea
NCTE Director of Publications

Teaching Writing as a Second Language

Alice S. Horning

WITH A FOREWORD BY W. ROSS WINTEROWD

Published for the Conference on College
Composition and Communication

SOUTHERN ILLINOIS UNIVERSITY PRESS
Carbondale and Edwardsville

Production of works in this series has been partly funded
by the Conference on College Composition and Communication of
the National Council of Teachers of English

Printed in the United States of America
Edited by Yvonne D. Mattson
Designed by Design for Publishing, Inc., Bob Nance
Production supervised by Natalia Nadraga

90 89 88 87   4 3 2 1

Library of Congress Cataloging-in-Publication Data

Horning, Alice S.
  Teaching writing as a second language.

  (Studies in writing & rhetoric)
  "Published for the Conference on College Composition
and Communication."
  Bibliography: p.
  1. English language—Rhetoric—Study and teaching.
2. English language—Study and teaching—Foreign
speakers. 3. Adult education. I. Conference on College Composition and Communication (U.S.) II. Title.
III. Series.
PE1404.H67   1987   808'.042'07   86-13043
ISBN 0-8093-1327-8

To my whole family, for support of various kinds
during the interminable writing and rewriting
of this book

Contents

Foreword
W. Ross Winterowd

SOME BOOKS, WHEN THEY APPEAR, ARE OBVIOUSLY SO RELEVANT, even essential, that we ponder our own shortsightedness in not having attempted to write them or not at least having anticipated them. Mina Shaughnessy's *Errors and Expectations* was one such book; its time had come, and it was part of Shaughnessy's genius to realize that historical exigency. Because *Errors and Expectations* problematized basic writing, it is irreplaceable.

Alice Horning's *Teaching Writing as a Second Language* is in the tradition started by Shaughnessy, taking basic writing not only as practical problem and a humane responsibility, but also as a challenging area for research and theorizing.

Since Horning interprets and applies the growing body of work in second language acquisition (for example, Larry Selinker's interlanguage hypothesis, John Schumann's research on pidginization, and Stephen Krashen's monitor theory), a less graceful but more informative title for this book might be *Principles and Theories of Second Language Learning and Teaching Applied to Basic Writing*. Not that Horning presents a literal translation of second language lore into dictates concerning the learning and teaching of written language—she is far too judicious for such enthusiasm. Hence, the book gains a second usefulness, as a critical review of mainline doctrines in second language scholarship, giving readers access to theories of language learning that are helpful, even essential, for teachers of writing. This practicality results not only from the territory that Horning has staked out, but from her admirably clear and accurate exposition. Into a relatively small number of pages, she has packed an enormous amount of information without leaving the reader panting and struggling to keep up with the development of her ideas.

The book is original because the author intelligently synthesizes her materials and applies them to basic writing, in Derrida's sense *supplementing Errors and Expectations.*

Alice Horning's *Teaching Writing as a Second Language,* like Mina Shaughnessy's *Errors and Expectations,* is worth, and hence invites, supplementation.

Acknowledgments

I WISH TO THANK THE FOLLOWING PEOPLE FOR CAREFUL READ-ings of many drafts of this manuscript: Linda Epstein, Van Hillard, Arthur Horning, Barbara Stone Reetz, and Ron Sudol.

I also wish to thank Kathy Zamora for typing the original draft of the text onto a word processor and James Malek for providing secre-tarial and other support services.

In addition, I thank Virginia Knight for a careful editing of a late draft of the manuscript, and for many changes of *which* and *that* I still don't understand, and thanks also go to Donald Morse for sup-porting part of Ms. Knight's work.

The chapters that concern the pidginization hypothesis and the monitor theory were read by Professors John Schumann and Stephen Krashen, respectively, and I am grateful to both for de-tailed comments on the arguments presented. Errors and omissions remaining are my responsibility.

Teaching Writing as a
Second Language

1

Toward a Theory of Writing Acquisition

MINA SHAUGHNESSY'S CLASSIC STUDY *ERRORS AND EXPECTATIONS* ushered in a period of intense research on the work of basic writers. Shaughnessy's work provided a much-needed catalog of the features of basic writing and the characteristics of the students who produce it, as well as an important chronicle of the events of the open-admissions years at the City University of New York. Despite its significance as the starting point for major research in basic writing, *Errors and Expectations* did not provide a cohesive, testable theory of writing acquisition. In the intervening years, many scholars and teachers have worked with basic writers, done research along the lines Shaughnessy suggested, and published their findings. The result is a patchwork of partial statements of theory, some of which make use of certain aspects of second language acquisition research but still do not provide either a comprehensive theory of writing acquisition specific to basic writers or a theory set up to be tested with continuing basic research. (In particular, Helmut Esau and Michael Keene discussed the relevant issues in the general context of college writing instruction in a 1981 *College English* essay. Stephen Krashen made similar proposals in 1984 in *Writing*.) This inquiry meets both of these goals.

The need for a comprehensive theory about basic writers has shaped the central hypothesis of this theory on writing acquisition, along with its corollaries. The theory must account for the largest possible body of data with the simplest and most elegant statements. In addition, the theory must make use of what we already

1

know about writing, and thanks to Shaughnessy and many others concerned with the rhetoric and psychology of writing, we know a great deal. The theory must account for both the written product, or "text," writers generate and the processes they use to do so. It must also account for the errors basic writers make. It must incorporate the role of affective factors that influence writers' behavior. And, finally, it must account for how these particular students make their way through the apprenticeship of basic writing courses in college and achieve proficiency in writing.

The central hypothesis of the theory states that basic writers develop writing skills and achieve proficiency in the same way that other adults develop second language skills, principally because, for basic writers, academic, formal, written English is a new and distinct linguistic system. This view rests in part on Shaughnessy's description of basic writers. They are usually adult beginners in college composition courses. While they have generally mastered the mechanical aspect of transcribing letters, they lack knowledge of both the specific rules of grammar and syntax and the broader conventions of organization and logic required in academic discourse. They are, moreover, newcomers to the academic community of a college or university, and while their native language may or may not be some dialect of English, formal written English is quite foreign to them. They must master both the language and culture of academia, and they face many of the same intellectual and psychological challenges that confront other second language learners.

Basic writers do acquire writing skills, and their progress and efforts are taken up in the theory in a series of six corollaries to the central hypothesis. These corollary claims are summarized here and then explored in detail in the chapters that follow. The first corollary is that the written form of language constitutes a second language. Studies over the last ten years have examined the nature of written language, especially in contrast to the spoken form. Several scholars have argued persuasively that written language is a distinct linguistic system. Spoken forms differ from written forms in a variety of ways, and these differences play a significant role in how students develop their writing skills. For basic writers (who, some scholars argue, are primarily from an oral culture), the difference between spoken and written forms is crucial to their writing and to the errors they make.

A second hypothesis states that, much like skill in a second language, writing skill develops through processes of acquisition and learning. Acquisition consists of a set of processes that are internally motivated, largely unconscious, yet systematic, but inaccessible to direct teaching. By contrast, learning results from a conscious effort to master clearly defined rules—an area in which teaching can make a critical difference. Basic writers develop a sense of the redundancy of language and proficiency in the written form through both processes of acquisition and learning. The claim that basic writers are engaged in *acquisition* requires much detailed study, but much of the research in second language acquisition suggests that certain aspects of acquisition are characteristic of basic writers.

The third hypothesis is that the acquisition of writing skills comes about in an ordered fashion. Although this ordering may be different from the kinds of "natural orders" found in first and second language acquisition, it still reveals a clear pattern. (The work of basic writers must be studied longitudinally and in detail to reveal the patterns, as in the case presented in chapter 5.) In many areas of psycholinguistic inquiry, researchers have found that if the data are studied long enough, an ordering ultimately appears. This point appears in the work of Mina Shaughnessy, Kenneth and Yetta Goodman, Frank Smith, Peter and Jill deVilliers, and many others. Much of the highly regarded work in psycholinguistics derives from the insight that acquisition takes place in an ordered fashion and that errors reveal the ordering. Teachers of basic writing need to understand that errors are essential to learning.

In a controversial statement, Stephen Krashen says that aspects of language that are learned function only as a monitor on the output of the acquired system. By extension, the fourth hypothesis claims that what students learn in the basic writing classroom functions only as a monitor on the output of the writing skills they have acquired. This point may help account for the problem of error, which aggravates teachers more than any other problem. Second language acquisition researchers have devised several ways of accounting for the phenomenon of error: according to Krashen, errors may result from nonoptimum use of the monitor, or perhaps from nonuse of the monitor altogether; they may derive from social or psychological distance between the learner and proficient users; and, alternatively, the errors may result because the process of acquisition may simply be at an intermediate stage ("interlanguage"). In addition, an analysis of errors in first and second language acquisition and in reading acquisition shows that errors result from the learner's systematic effort to master the redundant aspects of the language system. Teachers must come to see errors in writing in the same way that these errors are viewed in first language acquisition, reading, and second language acquisition: as a positive, essential characteristic of the task of mastering redundant language features.

A fifth hypothesis in the theory of writing acquisition is the input hypothesis of monitor theory, which states that "comprehensible input" is essential if language acquisition is going to take place. Comprehensible input must have certain characteristics that facilitate language acquisition. Krashen believes that comprehensible input contains understandable material somewhat beyond the acquirer's present level, varies in character, requires presentation in enormous quantities, reduces the acquirer's affective filter, and occurs in the context of natural language use.

Basic writing teachers can present input that contains amply varied material just beyond their students' present level from an abundant assortment of available texts, exercises, and other materials. The input hypothesis also suggests that basic writers must be presented with comprehensible input in huge quantities, and this point may suggest why many basic writing students do not succeed. Students probably do not get sufficient quantity in a composition class that meets for an hour a day, three times a week. By "large quantity," Krashen means truly enormous quantities of comprehensible input; perhaps basic writing classes ought to be arranged in the same way that second language classes are, that is, meeting every day for at least an hour, or more.

Finally, the input hypothesis claims that comprehensible input must occur in the context of natural language use, the same claim that occurs in the literature on composition. In articles in *College English, College Composition and Communication*, the *Journal of Basic Writing*, and other places, researchers have repeatedly pointed out that writing assignments must have some real meaning for students if they are going to be of use. Real writing for real audiences is part of Linda Flower's goal in her successful text *Problem-Solving Strategies for Writing* (which is not, however, aimed at basic writers). Thus, Krashen's point that acquisition demands natural language use applies to writing acquisition just as it does to second language acquisition.

The sixth and final hypothesis concerns the affective filter, which taps all of the learner's feelings and attitudes about the subject under study. In basic writers, an affective filter operates as it does in other second language learners: the affective filter must be down (not operating) in order for students to acquire writing skills. We do not yet know which affective factors form the filter for basic writing students or how to reduce the effect of the affective filter among these students. Basic writing students are "strangers in a strange land" and must be treated accordingly. By doing so, we may be able to reduce their affective filter. Articles in research journals dealing with students, in class and in conference, suggest ways of tearing down the walls that students sometimes build between themselves and their instructors. Anyone who has seen the glassy-eyed look of the basic writer in class knows the reality of the affective filter hypothesis and seeks ways to reduce that filter.

These six hypotheses are concerned with phenomena familiar to all basic writing teachers and represent an attempt to develop a cohesive theory of writing acquisition that incorporates the redundancy of language and facilitates the process of acquisition. Each of these hypotheses requires empirical studies of basic writing students, and these studies will either confirm or refute each point. The theory that writing is a second language accounts for many aspects of basic writers' behavior not explained by other theories. The following chapters explore this theory in detail to serve as a basis for experimental confirmation. At this point, teachers and researchers concerned with basic writers lack a theory to explain the behavior of these writers in class. Second language acquisition research analyzes many features of language learning and use that are shared by basic writers. Coupled with research showing that written language is distinct from spoken language and with research on the important psycholinguistic feature of redundancy in written language, these analyses support the central hypothesis of this proposal: basic writers learn to write as other learners master a second language because, for them, academic written English is a whole new language.

In what follows, the theory of writing acquisition is explored in detail. The chapters fall into three distinct units. Chapters 2 and 3 on spoken and written language and on redundancy provide the theoretical basis for the argument that academic discourse is a separate linguistic system characterized by particular psycholinguistic features. Chapters 4 and 5 present a detailed analysis of the behavior of basic writers with respect to the written form, reviewing both pertinent second language theory about learners' errors and a case study of one writer who reveals his progress as his writing ability develops over a term. Chapters 6 and 7 discuss the relevant affective factors as analyzed in second language acquisition theory and detail Stephen Krashen's recent proposals for a comprehensive theory of second language acquisition, which provide an important springboard for this comprehensive theory of writing acquisition. Chapter 8 reviews the entire theory, summarizes the evidence, and outlines the agenda for further research.

2

Spoken versus Written Language:
A Distinction

A RECENT ARTICLE IN THE *CHRONICLE OF HIGHER EDUCATION*
notes that enrollment in developmental courses, particularly in
writing, has increased in the last ten years (Evangelauf 3). That fact
comes as no surprise. The demand for developmental writing has
grown and continues to grow because so many students come to college while they are still acquiring writing skills. The hypotheses
below examine the nature of the acquisition process among these
writers. But prior to that, two concepts constitute the base of the
argument that, for basic writers, learning to write means learning a
whole new language. This chapter takes up the first of these concepts, which states that the written form of language is a distinct
linguistic system, a theorem supported by abundant research data.
Although this claim is controversial, strong evidence suggests that
writing's uniqueness derives not only from its psycholinguistic characteristics but also from its historical and educational significance.

In linguistic discussions, the spoken form is generally considered
the primary form of the language. However, a substantial body of
evidence suggests that the written form may represent more completely the language itself as well as a particular person's capability
with the language. Merald Wrolstad discusses these questions in "A
Manifesto for Visible Language." Wrolstad examines the evidence
for the primacy of speech and finds it weak. Instead, Wrolstad
believes that the written or visible language yields a much better
representation of human capacities with language. Following critic
Jacques Derrida, Wrolstad claims that meaning is often much more

thoroughly explicated in written language than in the conventional uses of spoken language. Wrolstad also finds written language more precise and efficient and therefore more in tune with the processing capacities of the brain. In looking at linguistic issues such as competence and performance, Wrolstad finds that the production of oral language rarely matches linguistic knowledge, a position repeated often in contemporary linguistic theory. Visible language performance, mostly in the form of writing, reveals one's linguistic competence more accurately. Finally, Wrolstad points out that, in studies of animal language acquisition, animals that have acquired a language sufficiently to communicate with humans have generally succeeded with the visible forms of language, that is, with sign language or some kind of visible signal system, rather than with audible language. On all these grounds, Wrolstad concludes that there is good evidence for a "primacy of written language" position, the primacy resting in writing's special ability to represent linguistic knowledge.

Writing is unique also because of its distinctive characteristics. Scholars concur on several important differences between writing and spoken language: the structure of the discourse in each, the mental processes at work, the distance of the audience, the role of editing, and the nature of change in the two forms. Writing and speech differ, first of all, in terms of language structure. Because writing makes use of recognized sections in the discourse, such as paragraphs, chapters, and whole books, it contains a more overt structure than spoken language. Frank Smith has pointed out that writing is adapted to reading so that writers produce text in a format that is convenient and helpful to readers (*Writing* 82–84). The structured nature of writing also permits a greater choice of linguistic and grammatical options and makes use of its own system for organizing and integrating ideas (de Beaugrande, *Text* 255–58). The markers of coherence in written text are another feature unique to writing, as discussed extensively by W. Ross Winterowd (301–9).

Written language may also be a unique mental system, related to but distinct from spoken forms. Patrick Hartwell argues persuasively for a "print code," citing evidence from Sternglass, Shaughnessy, and other researchers on basic writing. The print code is a part of the cognitive system and includes both surface forms and underlying strategies and style (Hartwell 23–24). The print code hypothesis predicts important features of basic writing that are illustrated in the case study in chapter 5. These include the contentions that errors beyond dialect interference and errors in reading are widespread among those who have not mastered the print code, that such errors tend to disappear in reading (as Bartholomae has shown), that writing competency develops separately from speaking, that structural forms in writing follow those of speech when the writer does not control print code, and that writing can only be learned by writing. Hartwell develops his hypothesis as an alternative to a dialect interference analysis of error in writing. His case is strong and supports the argument that written language is a distinct system— an argument that is supported by considerable additional evidence.

Writing is also distinct from speech because of its distance from the audience. In conversation, the speaker's audience is present and can respond, asking questions or using other nonverbal means to indicate a lack of understanding. Writing, however, is private and solitary (Nystrand 83), and usually the writer has no way to check on whether the meaning intended is the meaning conveyed. Thus, the distance from the audience makes writing inherently more difficult (Smith, *Writing* 69–77). This difficulty, in part, lies in the amount of information which the receiver can handle (de Beaugrande, *Text* 273). Consider, for example, the difference between hearing a written paper read out loud and listening to an informal talk on the same topic. The written paper, as readers of this text who have been to academic meetings can verify, imposes a hefty processing load, because it follows the constraints of writing rather than those of talk. By contrast, an informal lecture or presentation on the topic will be much easier to follow because it may allow for interaction between speaker and hearer or at least frees the speaker to respond to puzzled looks on audience faces, should they appear. The spoken form consists of dialogue, whereas writing consists of monologue (Collins 84–86).

Students just beginning to acquire written language may also run into trouble because writing requires editing for perfection, whereas speech does not. Shaughnessy noted:

> While many of their [basic writers'] problems with written English are obviously linked to the accidents of transcription in an unfamiliar medium, others seem to be rooted in real differences between spoken and

written sentences, differences that are exaggerated when the writer's own speech is non-standard but are there for the standard speaker as well. . . . Speech is more likely to follow normal word order and to tolerate a high level of redundancy and loose coordination. . . . Writing, however, withholds the utterance in order to perfect it. (51)

Although Smith contends that editing writing makes it easier because editing allows for greater precision of meaning (*Writing* 69–77), Robert de Beaugrande has considerable data showing that this easiness may not be much help to basic writers. De Beaugrande correctly points out that basic writers are unfamiliar with editing techniques that might allow them to achieve greater precision, and thus they find their writing plagued by problems resulting from carrying over oral forms to written text. "At least some specific writing problems are influenced by speech habits: speech pauses confusing punctuation; word sounds interfering with spelling; fuzzy boundaries of speech statements encouraging sentence 'errors'; and so on" (de Beaugrande, *Text* 257). De Beaugrande's findings show that the difference between spoken and written language has pedagogical implications that can be applied directly in the classroom. And basic writers need to develop skills that allow them to convert spoken forms into the conventions of written language. Although this matter will be discussed more fully in connection with Linda Flower's research, the pedagogical implications of the distinction are clear, and De Beaugrande's new text *Writing Step by Step* makes good use of his findings.

The pedagogical implications are clear even in the face of the findings of Farr and Janda (1985) concerning a speaker of vernacular black English (VBE). Although these researchers found that their subject did not carry his VBE forms or other characteristics of orality into his writing, they acknowledge that he might have been atypical in a number of ways. Moreover, they identify his problems in writing as those having to do with the logic and structure of written language—just those features under discussion here which make writing distinctive. The features that cause problems for the writer in Farr and Janda's study are rather similar to some of those found by Bartholomae in his case study. And Bartholomae correctly observes that writing is a separate linguistic system for basic writers.

Just as editing differences separate writing from speech, the nature of change helps to distinguish the two forms. Several scholars have observed that writing is consistent over time and space so that neither regional variants nor changes in pronunciation and syntax over time have made a signficant difference in English since the seventeenth century (Bereiter 73–93). But with such consistency has also come an important resistance to change in written forms that is not found in spoken language. The readiness of spoken language to admit new forms shows, for example, in cable television's "Sniglets," while writing's resistance to change can be seen in the great to-do over Webster's Third Unabridged and its "shocking" inclusion of many previously colloquial and nonstandard words. Writing's conservative nature marks it as different from spoken language, different enough for the present argument to qualify it as a separate linguistic system.

The historical perspective casts additional light on the differences between spoken and written forms. As Walter Ong and David Olson note, our literate society developed from a society that functioned wholly on an oral basis for quite a long time. Like Emig and other writers in composition theory, Ong and Olson both believe that the written form of language is a distinct language system. They also concur with the differences noted between the spoken and written forms outlined above. David Olson makes an essential distinction between a language he calls "utterance" and a language he calls "text" ("Languages of Instruction" 65–89). He asks whether the meaning is within the language itself, as is the case in "text," or whether the meaning is somewhat extrinsic to the language, in which case it is an "utterance." Our literate society has developed from utterance to text. Linda Flower has concisely summarized Olson's work, stating that "the history of written language has been the progressive creation of an instrument which could convey complete and explicit meanings in a text. The history of writing is the transformation of language from utterance to text—from oral meaning created within a shared context of a speaker and listener to a written meaning fully represented in an autonomous text" ("Writer-Based Prose" 268–92). Flower presents this summary of Olson's work in her discussion of writer-based prose, which reflects the development of writing from utterance to text. Perhaps, the process of basic writers developing writing skills mirrors the development of literacy in our society, as Olson's "ontogeny recapitulates philogeny" line of reasoning implies:

> Let us consider the origin of the assumption that the meaning is in the text and the implications of that assumption for language use. The assumption regarding the autonomy of texts is relatively recent and the language conforming to it is relatively specialized. Utterance, language that does not conform to this assumption, is best represented by children's early language, oral conversation, memorable oral sayings, and the like. Text, language that does conform to that assumption, is best represented by formal, written, expository prose statements. My central claim is that the evolution both culturally and developmentally is from utterance to text. ("From Utterance to Text" 262)

Actually, the distinction between spoken and written language is nowhere near as clear cut as all these writers would have us believe. Walter Ong has investigated the distinction between literacy and orality and has written about it extensively. Ong traces the development of literacy, particularly in American society, and points out that literacy was originally orally based; that is, one learned to read in order to speak well. In the oral basis of current culture, Ong distinguishes between primary and secondary orality: primary orality is "the pristine orality of mankind untouched by writing or print" and secondary orality is "induced by radio and television, and it is by no means independent of writing and print but totally dependent on them" ("Literacy and Orality" 41–42). Our writing students who come from an oral culture (either a primary or secondary oral culture) come from a world organized differently from the academic world, which is fundamentally a literate culture. According to Ong, students need to be shown the differences between primary and secondary orality and writing.

Ong also points out that the written form represents a technological achievement. Writing requires analytic, sequential, and linear thought and development, whereas oral forms use different styles of thought. Writing, therefore, opens up a new world to students from either a primary or secondary oral culture. This aspect of Ong's analysis suggests that writing students are essentially "strangers in a strange land" and must be assisted accordingly. In an anecdote, he describes the strange-seeming statements of a student from an oral culture trying to function in the written culture of academia. However, the student's statements seem no more peculiar than those of second language students trying to express themselves in a new language (42–43). The distinction between the spoken and written form has surely attracted all this attention in part because it tells us what kinds of needs our students in writing courses may have.

If we accept that the spoken form and its written form are distinct language systems, then the written form is probably a discrete language in and of itself that is learned by basic writers as a second language. The scholarly work discussed here thus far contends that writing is a second language for many students, a contention that opens up many possibilities for drawing on research in second language acquisition. In his 1966 essay "Written English Is a 'Second Language,'" Robert L. Allen was among the earliest to claim that the written form should be viewed as a second language (348–57). Allen asks for a complete description of written English and an equally complete description of spoken English in order to determine the similarities and differences. Linguistic research has moved in this direction, but the present descriptions of language are still not complete. Later writers ignored Allen, probably because linguistic research was not adequate to support his claims. Recent research, however, suggests that Allen's claims were perfectly correct. Esau and Keene's work supports all of Allen's claims as well as those made in this book. Dramatic advances in second language acquisition research have been made at an astonishingly rapid pace and have become increasingly relevant to the teaching of writing.

In *Errors and Expectations*, Mina Shaughnessy assumes that the written form of English needed by college students is for most equivalent to a second language, whether or not English is their native language. Shaughnessy also believes that basic writers are in alien territory when they set out to master formal written English.

> Not only may they feel constrained by the academic situation to shift registers, they may enjoy the sound and look of the new words and more elaborate phrasings of the unfamiliar register. To add to one's stock of words—more particularly to appropriate for one's own use the formidable jargon of the "others"—can be a gratifying kind of acculturation as well as a strategy for survival. . . . Learning is a sequence of approxima-

tions, some of them quite far from the intended mark, and it is not un-
usual for a student to sound worse before he sounds better. (194)

Acculturation is a process of getting used to being in a new society
with a new social and linguistic structure. Many student writers
must not only acculturate to the academic setting but also adapt to
the formal academic language required of them.

Writers must make a transition from producing a text that is a
kind of internal monologue to producing a text that can communicate ideas to other people. In her discussions of "writer-based
prose," Linda Flower examines this acculturation process. Flower's
research shows that as students begin to develop their abilities with
the written form, they move through several different levels or
styles. She makes a distinction on this basis between writer-based
and reader-based prose. "Writer-Based is a verbal expression written by a writer to himself and for himself. . . . In contrast, Reader-
Based prose is a deliberate attempt to communicate something to a
reader. [It] . . . creates a shared context, . . . offers a rhetorical
structure. . . . In its language and structure, Reader-Based prose
reflects the *purpose* of the writer's thought; Writer-Based prose
tends to reflect its *process*" ("Writer-Based Prose" 269). Thus, not
only is the written form a distinct language from the spoken form,
but, even within the written form, we find different bases for prose.

Flower illustrates the differences between writer- and reader-
based prose in an experiment in which people were asked to describe the layout of their apartments (for a sociological survey, they
were told). Most people used a tour style with narrative explana-
tions of the arrangement of the rooms rather than describing the
layout as one would describe a map, following a broad outline with
relevant details. The tour/narrative strategy is a good way to search
one's own memory, but it is very difficult for listeners to understand.
As Flower says, the tour strategy is writer-based, not reader-based,
and writer-based prose is much closer to oral forms than reader-
based prose ("Writer-Based Prose" 281). Flower's work implies that
the acquisition of reader-based prose (learning to write) is the process of acquiring a new language.

In an essay entitled "The Languages of Instruction: The Literate
Bias of Schooling," David Olson makes the same point for younger

students. He notes that the language used in school is a specialized language distinct from the child's native language. And the problem for children in school, which in some cases persists through college, is to master the special language of the schools:

> I have tried to show that explicit prose is a specialization of language serving a very limited number of functions extremely well, particularly those involved in description and explanation. Because it is a specialized form of language, it is not a mother tongue. Here then is our dilemma. The child comes to school, the master of a mother tongue, but the dominant means of instruction and communication in the school is the language of formalized written prose. All children have some difficulty moving into that special language, and some children find it largely inaccessible. (76)

Brooke Neilson disputes this claim in her doctoral dissertation. Neilson studied acquisition of the written form and questions the assumption that learning to write is like learning a second language. Her subjects, mostly white middle-class students at the University of California at San Diego, wrote texts that she analyzed. This population is not typical of basic writers. However, Neilson's study shows that these writers make many of the same types of errors that basic writers make. She finds a distinction between a "formal" register and an "informal" register and discovered that her subjects generated errors only when writing in the formal register. Neilson suggests that the errors are evidence of a performance problem and not a problem in language acquisition.

> First, errors occur in structures which writers use in both formal and informal registers, but only when such structures are used in formal register. Thus, the structures must be in some sense mastered, at least within the context of informal discourse; otherwise, errors should occur whenever the structures are used.
> Second, errors, if they indicate unmastered structures, should map well onto the differences between registers. That is, formal errors should occur in places where there are marked differences in the structures used in the two registers. In fact, however, the fit between error and register difference is not good. (140–41)

Neilson is suggesting that the student has partially mastered the structures of the formal register but not sufficiently to write well in that register.

This conclusion is probably a sound one for Neilson's population. But Olson might respond by saying that students at San Diego have at least partially mastered the "text" needed for schooling and that their problems with the written form may be a problem of performance, as Neilson suggests. A different population, however, more like the population of basic writers that Mina Shaughnessy describes in *Errors and Expectations*, would probably not come to the writing classroom with the "text" forms even partially mastered, finding it "largely inaccessible" as Olson suggests. Therefore, while Neilson's claim is correct for her population, the claim that writing is a second language for *basic* writers remains unchallenged (Cayer and Sacks 121–28).

Among basic writers, acquisition of the written form of language shares a number of characteristics with the development of skill in any other second language. The abundant literature in the psychological and linguistic theories that underlie composition pedagogy demonstrates that the written form of language which we expect students to know or to master in the first year of college is a distinct linguistic system, sufficiently different from spoken language to qualify as a distinct language. As a distinct language, it is acquired in a fashion similar to the acquisition of more traditional second languages: French, Spanish, German and the like. Therefore, insights from second language research can be successfully carried over and applied to the acquisition of writing ability. Now that we have established the differences between the spoken and the written systems, the written form can be scrutinized for its unique character.

3

The Role of Redundancy in the Acquisition of Written and Spoken Language

WRITTEN LANGUAGE IS A DISTINCT LINGUISTIC SYSTEM BECAUSE it makes extensive use of the psycholinguistic feature of redundancy to get messages across. Redundancy is particularly important in written language because of audience distance, as it helps ensure that messages are sent and received accurately. In addition, as the source of many errors made by basic writers, redundancy figures prominently in the present discussion. To master written language, basic writers must master redundancy. Redundancy is essential for both the comprehension and production of language, but it is perceived before it is produced. In developing an awareness of redundancy, learners formulate rules about various aspects of it and then test those rules, making errors in the process. Thus, first and second language acquisition and the acquisition of reading and writing ability are of necessity alike, because all involve the process of mastering the redundancy of language. By defining redundancy, examining its role in acquisition, and studying how learners master it and how teachers can teach it, we can demonstrate the importance of redundancy to basic writing.

Most people think of redundancy as repetition, and, usually, redundancy in this sense has a negative connotation. In the psycholinguistic sense, redundancy is quite different: it is a necessary and naturally occurring characteristic of language that ensures accurate information transmission from person to person. Simply defined, redundancy is information overlap in language. While the overlap may come from simple repetition, it more likely results from subtle syntactic and semantic characteristics. An example of syntactic redundancy is found in a sentence such as "The teachers were grading their papers," in which the plurality of the subject is conveyed by the -s ending, by the plural verb form *were*, and by the plural pronoun *their*. In case the reader or listener misses the plural marker on the subject, either the verb or the pronoun will convey the same information about the subject's plurality. In acquiring language, whether spoken or written, learners must master the redundancy of the language if they wish to ensure an information exchange. In this sense, redundancy is a positive and necessary feature of the communication capacity of language.

Redundancy's importance in all aspects of language acquisition emerges clearly from a detailed definition of the term. One analysis, provided by H. J. Hsia, a communications researcher, divides redundancy into syntactic, semantic, and pragmatic types. In Hsia's terms, syntactic redundancy is the overlap of information that derives from grammatical forms, endings, or markers providing the same information in several different places within a sentence. Semantic and pragmatic redundancy are much more complex. Hsia defines semantic redundancy as information overlap in the substance of the text, rather than in its grammatical form. Semantic redundancy might be said to exist at a lexical level, a sentence level, and a discourse level. At the lexical level, semantic redundancy exists in a word like "taxicab," where either taxi or cab conveys the meaning, and together there is an overlap (Hsia 77). At the sentence level, redundancy exists when a clarification or an example is given within the sentence so that the same idea is presented more than once. In the sentence "Redundancy, that is, information overlap, occurs when the same idea is presented more than once," the *that is* segment sets up a within-sentence semantic redundancy. This sentence-level redundancy might also be found in a pair of sentences in which the second sentence restates the concept of the first sentence in different terms. Discourse-level redundancy is semantic redundancy that derives from the overall structure of a longer piece of text. In one standard formula for essays, for instance, writers are encouraged to state their point in the opening, elaborate the point in the development paragraphs, and repeat the point at the end.

Several restatements of the point create broad semantic redundancy in the discourse as a whole.

Hsia's third category is pragmatic redundancy, which derives from the meaning attached to the language by the receiver of the message. Pragmatic redundancy might be considered as the information overlap that occurs between the message contained in the language itself and the knowledge that the receiver already has about the message. In studies of redundancy in reading and in psycholinguistic analyses of reading such as Frank Smith's *Understanding Reading*, the reader's prior knowledge of the information in the text is considered crucial in getting meaning from the printed page. Prior knowledge, or pragmatic redundancy, is the force of all experience that the receiver of a message has had, both real and vicarious, and both linguistic and substantive (that is, experience with language and experience with the way the real world functions). One study that looked at prior knowledge as measured by readers' free associations with substantive words from a passage showed that more prior knowledge aids in the recall of a passage (Langer and Nicolich). Although both semantic and pragmatic redundancy are very difficult to measure precisely, all three types of redundancy—syntactic, semantic, and pragmatic—are essential to communication. In part, then, knowing a language is knowing about the redundancy in that language and how to utilize or manipulate it to communicate with other language users. As a defining characteristic of language, redundancy is one of the properties of language that users must acquire if they are to use the language with proficiency.

Not only is redundancy essential to proficient language use, but it also shares other characteristics of acquisition: like other acquisition, redundancy develops unconsciously, is understood more readily than it is produced, results from hypothesis forming and testing, and evolves as a byproduct of real language use. The unconscious character of redundancy plays a role in all aspects of language acquisition. Language users are not normally conscious of the presence of redundancy although they make extensive use of it. Children focusing on the past-tense endings of verbs, for example, are mastering a feature of syntactic redundancy, and they are generally unconscious of this fact and of all the other aspects of acquisition.

One of the commonplace observations about language acquisition is that comprehension seems to be far ahead of production. In second language acquisition, this point emerges quite clearly. For the teaching of second languages, a teaching strategy known as "Total Physical Response" has been developed around the fact that learner comprehension is superior to production (Asher 79–84). In this type of teaching, students listen to and act on commands in the second language, developing their comprehension ability to an advanced level before they are expected or allowed to speak. Research studies demonstrate the success of this method. The "Total Physical Response" approach captures the similarity between first language acquisition and second language acquisition. In first language acquisition, children do extensive listening before they begin to produce recognizable language sounds.

Research in first language acquisition (deVilliers and deVilliers) and in reading and writing also supports the fact that comprehension is superior to production. Some of the early research of Kenneth and Yetta Goodman on miscue analysis shows that, in reading, comprehension is typically superior to oral performance. One of the Goodmans' favorite tales involves a child reading a story called "Space Pet," which is about two astronauts who smuggle a canary aboard a spaceship. The canary's collapse saves the astronauts' lives because its collapse indicates a malfunction in the oxygen system on the spaceship. The child read the entire story aloud and skipped the word *oxygen* every time it appeared in the story. When the child was asked to summarize the story, he said that the canary saved the astronauts' lives because it showed them that there was not enough *air* on the spaceship. As the Goodmans have pointed out repeatedly, children may not produce a word in oral reading, but such skips, mispronunciations, or other miscues do not necessarily show a failure to comprehend. Indeed, in most such cases, comprehension is far superior to what oral production might lead an observer to think.

A third characteristic found in language acquisition and redundancy is the use of hypothesis testing, and the errors that accompany such testing. Language acquisition takes place through a process of formulating and testing hypotheses about the rules of language. The learner must receive feedback on these hypotheses and continuously modify them until they match those of other people using the same system. Hypothesis testing and feedback concentrate on precisely those features of language that are redundant in nature. In the course of carrying out the hypothesis testing process, language users inevitably commit errors. These errors reveal the user's rules and usually occur on the redundant features of the language. As people learn to use language, they focus ordinarily on the meaning of the message being sent or received and not on its linguistic or grammatical form. The focus on meaning, common to all aspects of language acquisition, is facilitated by the redundancy present in language.

Finally, an awareness of redundancy evolves through experience with real language use. Children acquiring a first language practice every time they say something. The mastery of the redundant features of language also requires practice, and, for basic writers, this means the opportunity to generate quantities of writing. Like children learning a first language, basic writers must produce a great deal, get feedback on their production, and produce more before they can incorporate the important redundant features of written language into their own production.

Many recent papers in the field of language acquisition compare a particular aspect of spoken language acquisition to an aspect of written language acquisition, and these discussions shed light on how learners master redundancy. For example, in "Language Acquisition and the Teaching and Learning of Writing," Julia Falk compares children's acquisition of their first language to the acquisition of writing skills among adult learners. Much work has also been done comparing and contrasting first language acquisition and second language acquisition (Roger Brown, ch. 2). All of these comparative essays concur on the unconscious nature of acquisition. As Falk notes, "natural language acquisition is an unconscious process that occurs without overt teaching and without specially prepared materials. Children cannot and do not learn to talk from any overt teaching by their parents or caretakers. In fact, it appears to be impossible to teach a child to talk. There are no known exercises that will enable a child in the holophrastic [one word] stage to develop more rapidly into a speaker capable of combining two words into a simple sentence" (439). First language acquisition, as Falk describes it, is not accessible to direct teaching and does not seem to go on at a conscious level of awareness. The same point holds for adults learning a second language (R. Brown, ch. 2), that is, second language acquisition is also thought to be, at least in part, an unconscious process.

Learners pass through a series of stages as they move toward proficiency in the second language. Their progress is unconscious and rule-governed (Selinker).

Surprisingly, the same comparison holds for the acquisition of skills in written language, whether reading or writing. Reading and writing acquisition occur in an unconscious and rule-governed way. In an article called "Learning to Read is Natural," Kenneth and Yetta Goodman have claimed that reading acquisition seems to begin much earlier than most of us might think and in a fashion that is as unconscious as the processes by which spoken language is acquired. The Goodmans write that learning to read is unconscious and not accessible to direct teaching. "Reading begins when children respond to meaningful printed symbols in a situational context with which they are familiar. The onset of this process probably goes as unnoticed as the time when children begin listening. Yet there is lots of evidence in the literature that suggests that children develop some kind of print awareness at a very early age without formal instruction" (144). Parents whose children learn to "read" the McDonald's sign at age three can verify this claim easily. Thus, learning to read is just as unconscious as learning a spoken language. Falk demonstrates that learning to write takes place unconsciously, too. Like other aspects of language acquisition, writing skills cannot be taught directly in the conventional sense but rather must be *acquired* by the language user. The well-known failure of many different approaches to the teaching of writing substantiates Falk's contention.

The redundant characteristics of language make the process of writing skill acquisition partially unconscious. Certain redundant features can be taught: for instance, the system of plural markers or the semantic redundancy of the standard essay format described above. But every writing teacher who has used grammatical or punctuation exercises in class knows that while it is possible to present those things in class, getting the learner to use that information in written production is not a necessary or even a usual result of the class presentation. Grammatical endings and punctuation are aspects of redundancy in language, and because redundancy is part of the unconscious system of language, its aspects—syntactic, semantic, and pragmatic—cannot be taught. Rather, they must be acquired through what Julia Falk calls "tacit internalization" (440). The more we focus on the learner and what the learner must know and must do in the process of mastering language, the more the characteristics of redundancy and the characteristics of the acquisition processes coalesce.

If written language is acquired in ways similar to spoken language, then the importance of reading to writing is that comprehension of reading material will necessarily be ahead of production in writing, just as it is in spoken language acquisition. Comprehension of written forms, through reading, is a prerequisite to the acquisition and development of writing. Basic writers often have difficulty acquiring writing skills because, in general, they have read very little. But reading is essential. "Reading the writing of others as preparation for one's own writing is not a phenomenon restricted to the novice writer, nor is it a culturally determined activity special to the American scene. Established professional writers rarely recount and proclaim the influence of writing courses they may have taken in high school and college. Instead, they cite the influence of other writers" (Falk 439).

Learners internalize patterns and principles of redundancy as they work with written language, in both reading and writing activities (Shaughnessy 87). These patterns and principles are acquired first through comprehension, and then used and tested in production. Thus, because redundant features of language must be taken in before they can be produced, comprehension precedes production. Knowing the learner's need to master redundancy, teachers will be more able to provide opportunities for basic writers to master composition successfully.

Successful language acquisition also requires forming and testing hypotheses or guesses about the ways in which language functions. In reading and writing, as well as in first and second language acquisition, learners employ the hypothesis testing procedure. In fact, the most important contribution of psycholinguistic theory and the Goodmans' miscue analysis lies in the insight that children learning to read make guesses about the way in which written language works. The miscues produced by children in oral reading reveal the rules or hypotheses they have set up, and these miscues are highly systematic. The Goodmans label children's oral changes in a written text *miscues* for the purpose of distinguishing them as positive, systematic, and distinct from errors. Learning to read is a process of figuring out the significant differences among the letters and/

or words and working out how they convey meaning. The Goodmans, and others who share their views, believe that knowing the names of letters and words has little to do with getting meaning from print. The essential aspects of these phenomena cannot be taught to children learning to read: instead, the children must master them through hypothesis forming and testing. Frank Smith describes the process by which this takes place: "No one can teach them directly what the relevant categories, distinctive features and interrelationships are, yet children are perfectly capable of solving the problem for themselves provided they have the opportunities to generate and test their own hypotheses and to get appropriate feedback. In quite a literal sense, learning to read is like learning spoken language" (*Reading* 179). Research literature on children learning to read shows clearly that children do generate hypotheses and use what appears on the printed page to test those hypotheses. In this way, the text is an important source of feedback and plays a key role in the hypothesis-testing process.

All aspects of spoken and written language acquisition involve hypothesis testing and feedback. In first language acquisition, children formulate and test rules for the grammatical, semantic, and pragmatic aspects of their language, and language users around them provide essential feedback. In second language acquisition, learners formulate hypotheses in the same manner, test them, often in classroom production situations, and get relevant feedback from other speakers and/or from an instructor. The evidence in second language acquisition is not quite as accessible as the evidence from children's oral reading, but there is more and more research being done in this area. Second language learners formulate rules about the second language they are studying and test them in production:

> The learner [is] looked on not as a producer of malformed, imperfect language replete with mistakes, but as an intelligent and creative being proceeding through logical systematic stages of acquisition, creatively acting upon his linguistic environment as he encounters its forms and functions in meaningful contexts. By a gradual process of trial and error and hypothesis testing, the learner slowly and tediously succeeds in establishing closer and closer approximations to the system used by native speakers of the language. (Brown, *Principles* 163)

All language is acquired through this hypothesis-testing and feedback system, and, given the opportunity, learners are able to conduct this testing on their own.

In the acquisition of writing skills, hypothesis testing plays a similar critical role. Writers formulate hypotheses about written forms and then test and revise their production in order to develop their own system of written language use. Writers must have an opportunity to test their writing out on readers and get feedback, particularly if they are basic writers. The scope of the opportunities needed and the nature of the most useful feedback are unclear and may be unattainable in current classroom settings. But the concept of the writing teacher as "coach" moves in this direction (Dawe and Dornan 1–23).

Many of the hypotheses tested by language users concern various aspects of redundancy. Consider, again, the -ed marker used in English to mark the past tense form of most verbs. In first language acquisition, children typically set up a rule that says "form the past tense by adding -ed." This rule works well for most regular verbs, but when a child encounters a verb like *to draw*, the rule is inappropriate. When the child tries to apply the "add -ed" rule, there will be feedback from other language users that the rule does not apply in this case. Similarly, in second language acquisition, learners must master the ways that the new language has for conveying information like tense forms.

The -ed marker is one of many word endings and other forms we use that can be syntactically redundant. The -ed marker is redundant, for example, when it is accompanied by a time adverbial expression (for example, *yesterday*). In writing, the -ed marker also presents a problem, precisely because it is redundant and because the past tense idea may be conveyed by other aspects of the text. Language learners, including writers, formulate hypotheses about the -ed marker and other redundant aspects of language. Feedback from proficient language users enables these learners to revise their hypotheses until they bring them into line with those of proficient users. Inevitably, errors occur in the process of hypothesis forming and testing. Errors have been the focus of much work in all aspects of language acquisition, especially in those aspects of language most frequently presented in classrooms. The most important insight derived from the research on errors shows that they are systematic in nature and occur as learners develop a coherent linguistic system. Basic writers also reveal this systematic development of a linguistic system. Mina Shaughnessy shows that, from the outset, basic writers do not make random errors in their use of written forms. If there are enough data, patterns appear, showing the systematic errors. The inappropriate forms used by writers in the early stages of writing acquisition are similar to the inappropriate forms used by children, second language learners, and those learning to read: they reveal the development of the acquirer's own system.

In all aspects of language acquisition, errors show that learners develop their own rule systems for the language or form they are acquiring, and the learners' rules are only gradually brought in line with the rules of proficient users. The rules share characteristics with the rules of other language systems: these error-filled productions are described as an idiosyncratic dialect (Corder, "Idiosyncratic Dialects" 100–113). The errors are systematic because they result from redundancy, which is systematic. Analyses of learner errors show that many errors occur at points when learners try to master redundant language features. For instance, among basic writers, Shaughnessy finds many errors in past-tense markers, in the apostrophe for possession, and in other syntactically redundant features of written language. Similarly, in first language acquisition, we have already noted children's propensity for forming a rule concerning the -ed past-tense marker. This marker is often syntactically redundant, given the content of the rest of the sentence. Recent work in error analysis in second language acquisition shows a similar systematic character to learner errors. The phenomenon of error in second language acquisition is so clearly recognized that researchers call it interlanguage (Selinker). Error analysis in second language research provides a helpful model that will be applied to the work of basic writers later on in this book.

Finally, for the acquisition of reading skills, the Goodmans' research shows a systematic character of oral reading errors, especially among beginning readers. Miscue analysis makes plain that children rely on the syntactic and semantic regularity of language to get meaning from print. Beginning readers' errors do not indicate an inability to comprehend but instead show their systematic efforts to use what they know about the language in order to comprehend.

A beginning reader's focus on meaning or comprehension is not surprising, because in all aspects of language use, the focus is on meaning. The young child learning a first language is naturally concerned with getting a message across to other language users. In second language acquisition, while classroom exercises may focus on form, second language learners must ultimately learn to get meaning into the language they are using and learning. In the acquisition of the written form of language, the same focus on meaning prevails. So, in learning to read, children must come to understand that print is meaningful. In the acquisition of writing, again, the classroom focus is often on form and elements of form in writing, but, sooner or later, the beginning writer and the proficient writer must learn to match the meanings in their heads with the words they have written on paper (Shaughnessy 187–89). Frank Smith emphasizes the importance of the meaningfulness of language in his discussion of the similarity between first language acquisition and the acquisition of reading skill:

> Reading *is* a matter of making sense of print, and meaningfulness is the basis of learning. The issue concerns how children might initially acquire the insight—or at least hypothesize—that print is meaningful, that differences in print make a difference in the world. And just as children must and do begin learning spoken language by finding that meaning can be brought to speech—before they have the language skills that would produce that speech—so it must be possible for children to test and prove the hypothesis that print is meaningful even before they are able to read a word. (*Reading* 182)

In all aspects of language acquisition, redundancy is the characteristic of language that ensures the transfer of meaning from person to person. The fact that redundancy is essential to the communication of meaning is pointed out by H. J. Hsia, who states that "redundancy is fundamental in communication. Without redundancy, no communication is intelligible; without redundancy, no natural language could have been developed" (63). Because redundancy plays this central role in all language acquisition, teachers will want to enhance learners' mastery of it by teaching formulas that build redundancy in writing, by providing hands-on experience, and by presenting "comprehensible input" in the classroom.

In the standard freshman composition course, first of all, college writing students must learn the expected format for essays, term papers, and similar pieces of writing. The format usually given to students is an exercise in redundancy. The standard essay formula builds broad semantic redundancy by telling the reader the point of the essay, stating the point in detail, and repeating the point or thesis at the end. This formula is helpful to students acquiring writing skills because it helps them formulate hypotheses concerning the way in which written language must be presented if it is to convey meaning. Redundancy, because it ensures that the meaning gets across, becomes one of the most important elements the writing student must learn. The presence of redundancy ensures that the meaning is conveyed from speaker to hearer, and from writer to reader. Thus, the similarity of focus on meaning comes as no surprise when redundancy is considered as the surety bond on meaning.

Learning about redundancy takes place as a result of "hands-on" experience with language. Thus, learners require infinite opportunities to practice the language or language form under study. Learning by doing comprises the chief activity in first language acquisition. Children learn to talk by talking and by trying to get their messages across to others. Probably the only way to learn to speak one's native language is by speaking it, by making errors, and by modifying the system until it parallels that used by proficient speakers. Similarly, skill in a second language develops not from extensive lectures about the language but from many opportunities for real language use. In reading acquisition, children must have many opportunities to come into contact with print and to make the connection between print and meaning if they are going to learn to read.

Writing teachers need to replicate these conditions for basic writers. This need creates a problem of simple logistics. Writing teachers know that students learn to write by writing and that, in fact, composing is the only way in which writing skills can be truly mastered. The classroom or the environment can provide a central source of relevant input for learners, even though they will acquire aspects of the language system at their own pace. Monitor theory in second language research shows that teachers can provide relevant input while acquisition takes place. Information about redundancy may be one type of relevant input, but there may be others that deserve attention.

The new computer technology promises to provide new ways to set up "doing" situations, particularly as it speeds the writing process for many students and facilitates and encourages revising. In a new book, Helen J. Schwartz provides many activities that encourage writers to write a lot and revise thoroughly and thoughtfully. As she points out, word processing's chief attraction is that it makes revising easy and neat. Thus, writing on word processors will increase the means of engaging in writing in fundamental ways. Until computers become widespread and accessible to basic writers, we must try to understand learners and their development process in language acquisition in order to facilitate it successfully. The use of language is the only way to develop a sense of its redundancy.

In addition to teaching students the application of redundancy in writing, teachers can provide learners with "comprehensible input" (Krashen), information that the learner can use to formulate hypotheses and to test them in the acquisition process. Teachers' most essential role may be to provide direct feedback as learners test hypotheses. Teachers can also engage in error analysis based on models from work in second language acquisition. Error analysis research may also tell teachers more about how to provide the right sort of input for learners to formulate hypotheses. Finally, teachers of second languages and teachers of writing can provide the "doing" situations that afford opportunities for real language use. Teachers who really understand what the learner is doing should be able to maximize practice, hypothesis testing, errors and feedback to help the learner. All of these elements are necessary for the acquisition of language and the mastery of the redundancy of language. Language acquisition has these characteristics because redundancy has these characteristics. In teaching writing, teachers must be aware of the fact that writers must master redundant forms and can only do this through exposure, practice, hypothesis testing, and feedback. Unsuccessful writing acquisition occurs when there is insufficient opportunity to master the redundancy of language. Research on second language acquisition shows that unsuccessful second language acquisition also occurs when learners do not have an adequate opportunity to learn about redundancy. For this reason, second language acquisition research contributes importantly to the development of a theory of writing acquisition.

The argument of these first two chapters concerns the language that basic writers are working to acquire. This language, academic written English, has been established as a distinct linguistic system, sufficiently different from the spoken form to be considered a separate language, as discussed in chapter 2. The characteristics of this language include, particularly, its patterns of psycholinguistic redundancy. Chapter 2 showed that this language is sufficiently different from spoken language to be considered a separate language, while in this chapter we have looked at shared features of all languages and language forms which create similarities in acquisition strategies. The next segment of the argument looks at the body of research in second language acquisition that addresses the question of learner error. Errors in second language learning that are systematic and rule-governed constitute the student's interlanguage. Chapter 4 considers the interlanguage hypothesis in detail and its relevance to the theory of writing acquisition. Chapter 5 applies the theory directly to the case of a basic writer and his errors over a term in a basic writing class.

4

Error Analysis:
The Interlanguage Hypothesis
Applied to Basic Writing

ONE MODEL OF SECOND LANGUAGE ACQUISITION THAT CAN BE profitably extended to basic writing is Larry Selinker's interlanguage hypothesis. This hypothesis can not only improve teachers' perceptions of basic writers' problems and their control, but can also improve teachers' attitudes toward errors in writing. The interlanguage hypothesis addresses the nature of second language learning from the learner's rather than the teacher's perspective. Selinker looks at what happens when students attempt to produce sentences in the new language. The students' sentences are generally somewhat different from those of native speakers under similar circumstances. Because of these differences, Selinker hypothesizes that second language learners pass through a stage of language ability in which systematic errors of various kinds occur. This stage Selinker calls the interlanguage. "Since we can observe that these two sets of utterances are not identical, then in the making of constructs relevant to a theory of second language learning, one would be completely justified in hypothesizing . . . the existence of a separate linguistic system based on the observable output which results from a learner's attempted production of a target language norm. This linguistic system we will call 'interlanguage'" (*New Frontiers* 117–18). Two important and attractive features of the interlanguage concept for writing teachers are that the interlanguage stage is systematic and that students move through interlanguage toward proficiency. Based on errors in both second language learning and in writing, the inter-language concept supports Shaughnessy's claim that the errors of basic writers are systematic (5). More importantly, however, the hypothesis provides a helpful framework in which to examine student writing errors. Interlanguage frequently manifests itself, as we will see in the work of GW (the subject in the case study reported in the next chapter), in the redundant features of written language. If the interlanguage hypothesis is applied to basic writing, teachers will see that errors represent an interlanguage stage in the development of writing skill and are indicative of progress rather than failure.

In the day-to-day teaching of composition, teachers know that errors are the most exasperating aspect of student writing. Classroom exercises, scolding, low marks, even logic and analysis, seem to do little to reduce the error rate effectively or to alleviate the student's or the teacher's feelings of frustration and helplessness. The inter-language hypothesis raises the possibility that error is a necessary and desirable feature of learning. The hypothesis casts student writing errors into a radically different and much more favorable light.

Among the issues that connect second language learning and learning to write is the ease or difficulty with which the learning is accomplished. For a very few people in the general population, language skill in a second language or in written language comes easily and effortlessly. For the majority of learners, however, in both second language and writing, explicit teaching is necessary. The explicit teaching in both cases involves the use of patterned drills. In second language teaching, students are drilled in pronunciation, in syntactic patterns, sometimes in idiom usage, and so on. Writing students are given exercises to help them learn punctuation, verb forms, or syntactic fluency through sentence combining. Although the drills are done differently, one result is the same in both cases. The students, with some practice, often perform flawlessly under drill conditions, but when asked to communicate orally or in writing, they fall apart.

The errors that appear when meaningful communication is attempted reveal two other important points of similarity between second language learning and learning to write. First, the goal in both learning situations is to be able to communicate well enough to interact with native speakers. Second language learners need to be able to communicate an idea to speakers of the target language, and writing students need to be able to get what they know on paper to pass an exam, get a job, write a letter, or fill out a form. A second shared feature lies in the errors learners make. In second language learning, errors appear from the very beginning, and some even persist after near-native proficiency is achieved. An acquaintance of mine, who is fluent in Japanese and English, still makes an occasional error in preposition usage, even though his English is flawless in every other way. Additionally, errors persist after drill in both cases and regardless of how much instruction the students receive on the point of the error.

Selinker suggests that the interlanguage errors of second language learners result from a process called fossilization. The concept of fossilization accounts for the reappearance of errors in learners' production, even when their drill performance is quite good.

> Fossilizable linguistic phenomena are linguistic items, rules and subsystems which speakers of a particular native language will tend to keep in their interlanguage relative to a particular target language, no matter what the age of the learner or amount of explanation and instruction he receives in the target language. . . . It is important to note that fossilizable structures tend to remain as potential performance, reemerging in the productive performance of an interlanguage even when seemingly eradicated. . . . Note that the claim is made here that, whatever the cause, the well-observed phenomenon of 'backsliding' by second language learners from a target language norm is not, as has been generally believed, either random or toward the speaker's native language, but toward an interlanguage norm. ("Interlanguage" 119)

Fossilization helps account for the fact that composition students can routinely make subjects and verbs agree or place apostrophes correctly in exercises but continue to make errors in writing. Fossilization occurs, according to Selinker's hypothesis, as a result of at least five central processes. Each of these processes applies equally to second language learning and to the learning of writing.

The first and most obvious process of fossilization among second language learners is language transfer. In this case, fossilization occurs as a result of the native language of the student. Language transfer may be the most obvious source of interlanguage behavior, and an example cited by Selinker makes clear what he means by language transfer. Suppose that a native speaker of German is trying to learn English. In German, word order rules dictate that time phrases precede place phrases following the conjugated verb. When this student attempts to create a sentence in English, the result might be "I will go at 1:00 to the bank," while the native speaker would say "I will go to the bank at 1:00." Second language teachers might recognize this as a translation problem and say that the student needs to learn to "think in" the second language.

Basic writers show language transfer when they attempt to translate from the spoken form with which they are familiar (it might be called their native language) to the special target language of formal writing. This transfer leads to errors of many types. One possible example is the use of "it is" for "there is" or "there are." In the spoken form, a student might say, "It's a lot of people going to the party," while in writing the required form is "There are a lot of people going to the party." The language transfer process may be the source of this type of error.

A second source of fossilization is the training the student has received: Selinker calls it transfer of training. In this case, the interlanguage behavior is created by a particular format used in teaching or training the student. For instance, a good many languages have the same pronoun distinctions as English, that is, male, female, and neuter. Selinker's example is drawn from a speaker of Serbo-Croatian who tended to use *he* rather than *he or she* in his English production because of the predominance of *he* in the textbooks and drills.

Transfer of training is less clear in the problems basic writers have, but may account for another phenomenon familiar to writing teachers. Basic writers may, for example, do just fine in their use of commas, perhaps omitting one or two that are required, but not making serious comma errors, until the comma rules are presented in class. The effect of training and exercises in comma use is that suddenly the students have serious comma errors of all sorts, and commas appear in their sentences where they never put them before. If the interlanguage hypothesis is correct, the appearance of many commas as a result of transfer of training is a form of fossilization in the writer's interlanguage and thus represents progress toward correct comma usage. Although teachers may be frustrated to see the errors, they actually provide strong evidence of the students' movement toward correct writing. While this chapter was being written, a student of mine provided a nice example of this transfer of training phenomenon in his comma usage. Before our class discussion of comma rules, he wrote:

> My friends have told me that I have a nice looking car.

Once we had covered commas, this student went a little comma crazy:

> When, I did see her about a month ago, she said it was all my fault that, we did not marry.

Later, his writing was still plagued by an overabundance of commas. My sense told me, however, that he was beginning to reduce the comma errors he made as he moved toward writing proficiency.

Two additional sources of fossilization are treated separately by Selinker, but since they are hard to distinguish, they can be examined together. Both relate to strategies used by the learner in attempting either mastery of, or communication in, the new language. For instance, the learner may try to reduce the target language to a simpler system, either because the target language is too complex or because the student realizes that certain features of the target language are redundant for native speakers. In this manner, a native English speaker attempting to learn German may leave case markers off words, since there are many more cases in German than in English. Chances are that the native speaker of German will be able to get the idea of the sentence just the same. Russian speakers learning English tend to avoid articles, plurals, and past tense forms, knowing that no native speaker of English would have trouble getting the point of sentences like these:

> It was nice, nice trailer, big one.
> I have many hundred *carpenter* my own.
> I *was* in Frankfort when I *fill* my application. (Selinker, *New Frontiers* 123)

The interlanguage hypothesis suggests that the learner applies specific strategies in an attempt to master the new language or in an attempt to communicate with native speakers of the new language. These strategies often involve simplifying or avoiding complexities, and, in both cases, the student produces interlanguage forms.

When basic writers are confronted with what must seem to be a fairly complex system of rules for the third-person-singular, present tense verb forms, they make a similar kind of effort to simplify the system. The errors tend to take two forms. Either the writer leaves off all of the -s markers on the verbs, or the -s appears not only in third person singular, but also in first and second person, and sometimes on the past-tense or plural verb forms as well. Here is one example from GW, who tried, at least, to be consistent with the -s. His system seems to be that if there is no -s on the subject, he puts no -s on the verb, and -s on the subject requires -s on the verb:

I enjoy the way my *car handle* on the road.

but

I have learned to make wiser *choices* that *makes* my next choice easier.

It is not a bad system, but it is not in line with current correct usage either. Toward the end of the term, as we will see below, he began to make fewer agreement errors of this type, but a rush job on a writing assignment revealed that he still had not eliminated this fossil.

As Selinker says, fossilization is always potentially present in performance, even after the interlanguage forms appear to have been eradicated by the student. The -s marker on verbs may be a most troublesome feature for basic writers just because their strategy of communication says that the message will get across with or without the -s. Again, the interlanguage forms or errors are an indication that the writer is trying to apply a strategy of learning or communication, not that he or she has no strategy or is stupid. The interlanguage hypothesis supports Shaughnessy's claim that writing errors are systematic in nature. Moreover, the errors indicate progress, because they show that the writer is producing interlanguage forms and moving toward proficiency in writing.

A final cause of fossilization is the overgeneralization of the rules of the target language. This is a common phenomenon in both second language acquisition and in children's acquisition of their native language. In English, the nonnative speaker might try to apply the rule for the formation of the past of regular verbs and say "What did he *intended* to say?" and children produce such forms as *falled* and *felled* as they attempt to sort out the rule and exceptions for past tense forms. Again, Selinker's hypothesis gives learners much credit, suggesting that they have learned the rule and now must only master a knowledge of the situations in which it applies. Overgeneralization fossils are perhaps the best sort of fossils to find, because overgeneralized rules are most often ones that reflect redundancy and because they do indicate that the basic principle has been mastered.

Because overgeneralization fossils show that the student has learned the rule, writing teachers ought to be encouraged rather than discouraged when they see student writers producing forms like *wented, six orange's,* and *hurries'*. These writers have learned that some past-tense forms must have the -ed ending and that the apostrophe has some use in English. These students need only learn the situations in which the rules apply and those in which the rules do not apply. There is an additional message here for the classroom teacher: once the rule has been learned, drill or practice can be focused on situations in which the rule does and does not apply. It is not necessary to continue teaching the rule.

Yet anyone who teaches basic writing already sees the flaws in the interlanguage hypothesis. Selinker admits to several of them, and they apply equally to second language learners and to writing students. First, there are additional sources of fossilization beyond those covered by the five central processes described by Selinker. Spelling pronunciation is one problem that creates fossilization by second language learners, and, in basic writing, one might say that "pronunciation spelling" is the cause of much spelling trouble. A student of mine who was a speaker of a nonstandard dialect of English had a lot of trouble believing that *athlete* did not have another *e* to reflect his pronunciation: *athelete*. In addition, it is not always possible to categorize an error as being unambiguously the result of one of the five central processes. The exact sources of fossilization in both second language learning and writing require further study. Despite these problems, the point of the interlanguage hypothesis, namely that errors reflect learner progress, remains valid.

Selinker does not explain why fossilization in any of its forms occurs, nor does he try to predict which forms will fossilize for a particular student. Recent evidence presented at a symposium on interlanguage, however, suggests that fossilization may be specific to certain discourse domains, one of which may well be academic written English. Selinker has suggested that discourse contexts might be particularly important in teaching writing, although not much is known about the effect of such contexts on fossilization (Selinker, "Current State" 335 and Selinker and Douglas, "'Context' in Interlanguage Theory"). However, the five processes he has identified provide a useful framework for sorting and analyzing data. The same points hold for writing students: we can sort the errors and begin looking at the data in an analytical fashion, which may lead to an understanding of the causes of fossilization.

An important contribution to such work was made in 1980, when David Bartholomae's "Study of Error" appeared. Bartholomae's analysis agrees quite fully with the argument presented here: basic writing can be usefully studied from the perspective of second language acquisition research, and, more specifically, basic writers produce language forms that constitute an interlanguage. Bartholomae examines in detail the work of one basic writer, John, and carries out an error analysis on John's writing. The results of the analysis demonstrate that John uses a number of forms that can be most generously described as "unconventional" (264), but that they can also be described in two other ways. First, they can be analyzed in terms of the writer's internally coherent system of rules governing his behavior. In addition, Bartholomae asked this writer to read his paper aloud and found that, in the reading, John corrected most of his errors in the written form. Such changes make clear that the writer is aware that written text must follow particular rules of grammar and rhetoric.

Bartholomae goes on to point out the significant pedagogical implications of his findings: using second language theory as a base, teachers can analyze errors as evidence of the writer's current system and can teach the writer to alter that system by using reading and editing techniques. Although "The Study of Error" does not reveal the reasons for fossilization, it provides additional evidence that fossilization occurs, and Bartholomae calls for additional large-scale studies of the errors of basic writers. He agrees at the end of his essay that basic writers pass through stages as they move toward writing proficiency, and the stages should be studied and charted.

He says that "the approximate systems they [basic writers] produce are evidence that they can conceive of and manipulate written language as a structured, systematic code. They are 'intermediate' systems in that they mark stages on route to mastery (or more properly, on route to conventional fluency) of written, academic discourse" (Bartholomae 257). Chapter 5 provides detailed evidence further illustrating the claim that basic writers pass through an interlanguage stage.

Bartholomae's contentions stand up even in the face of other evidence suggesting that basic writers who are speakers of nonstandard English do not show evidence of fossilization resulting from the influence of their native dialect. Evidence of this kind is presented in the case study by Farr and Janda that appeared in 1985. They found that "neither VBE (Vernacular Black English) patterns in the student's oral language nor other features of orality which previous research has identified primarily account for his writing problems" (62). However, they note that their student may not be representative of basic writers in general, nor of beginners in particular. A number of points suggest that he is not typical: he has had other work in composition, does not show many surface errors in his writing, belongs to a family that has moved upward socioeconomically, and lives on the campus at his school. For all these reasons, this student fits neither Shaughnessy's classic profile of basic writers nor, particularly, the beginning basic writer under discussion here. Thus, Bartholomae's claims, like Selinker's and the others we've discussed, are good evidence to support the claim that basic writers move through an interlanguage stage on their way to writing proficiency.

The most puzzling problem Selinker admits to being unable to solve is the issue most teachers really want help on: how does the learner move from interlanguage to proficiency in the target language? When Selinker first proposed the interlanguage hypothesis, a complete description of even one interlanguage was not available, and the processes learners use to move from the interlanguage to proficiency were inaccessible. In this connection, Roger Andersen's work on pidginization and interlanguages is helpful. Andersen views the development of the interlanguage as a salient step in language acquisition that is of great inherent significance. Andersen sees interlanguage development as part of two interacting forces in the course of acquisition:

Nativization is the composite of processes by which an individual language learner creates an internal representation of the language he is acquiring and the subsequent assimilation of the new input to the learner's gradually evolving internal representation of that second language. *Denativization* is the gradual restructuring of the learner's somewhat unique and idiosyncratic internal representation of the language he is acquiring in terms of the input he processes during language acquisition. Nativization proceeds away from the target input; denativization towards it. ("One to One" 78)

Andersen goes on to say that nativization does not particularly move learners away from the target language so much as it moves them to an independent system that, as one of its key features, is "internally consistent" (79). Learners employ, according to Andersen, a "one to one principle" (79) in the construction of their independent interlanguage system. "The One to One Principle specifies that an IL system should be constructed in such a way that an intended underlying meaning is expressed with one clear invariant surface form (or construction). . . . The 1:1 Principle is thus a principle of one *form* to one *meaning*" ("One to One" 79). Clearly, not all of these features apply to basic writers, but the general idea of building a system that has internal consistency and that makes straightforward unitary connections between form and meaning is well supported in the case presented in the next chapter.

Andersen goes on to note that this does not help answer the question of how learners move from interlanguage to proficiency, but he does offer one interesting bit of speculation. Early changes in the rules of the interlanguage seem to revolve around the use of the system of auxiliary verbs, having to do with negatives, tense, aspect, and the like. These changes come about as forms and meanings become more complex and more interrelated. Like second language researchers, researchers in basic writing may want to look at the development of individual grammatical forms to see if they hold the key to how learners move toward proficiency in the target system. Such studies should, according to Andersen, involve case studies and cross-sectional as well as longitudinal research.

Before we can go on to the case study, attention must be drawn to two additional, serious problems with the interlanguage hypothesis. First, it does not fit together in any specific way with any particular linguistic theory, nor is there evidence of the psychological validity of the hypothesis. Moreover, since interlanguage represents a stage that learners go through as they move from incompetence to proficiency, longitudinal studies will be needed to investigate the hypothesis among both second language learners and basic writers. Bartholomae and Andersen agree on this, as noted above. In writing, some studies of this sort are only now beginning, and it will be some time before the relevant data become available.

While the data are accumulated and the basic research is being carried out, the interlanguage hypothesis has much to offer to the teacher of basic writing. Initially, it provides an explanation of the source of some student errors, particularly if the analogy between learning to write and learning a second language is kept in mind. Students of basic writing, just like second language learners, show fossilization due to language transfer, transfer of training, strategies of learning and communication, and overgeneralization. Although we do not yet fully understand how fossilization arises or how learners in either field move from interlanguage to proficiency, the nature of the system and the learners' perception of it are under study. Many learners clearly do move through the interlanguage stage that Selinker proposes. When basic writers move to the interlanguage stage in their learning, teachers ought to recognize their errors, particularly on redundant elements, as progress toward proficiency, rather than as evidence of failure. If teachers' attitudes towards error can be improved, writing students will be able to move more quickly and easily through interlanguage to writing proficiency.

5

"Good" Errors:
A Case Study in Basic Writing

THE INTERLANGUAGE HYPOTHESIS PROPOSES A STAGE LEARNERS pass through as they move toward language proficiency. Basic writers show characteristics of an interlanguage stage, along with other behavior similar to that of second language learners. Second language research on errors has much relevance to errors in basic writing. A detailed study of errors made by one writer shows that many of the findings of second language researchers on the stages of errors, their types, and their resolution are helpful in basic writing.

Stephen Krashen has observed that adults developing skill in a second language use strategies common among children as well as those found in formal, conscious learning, which most teachers hope are utilized in classes. "They can *acquire* naturally, which means language acquisition similar to child language acquisition, or they can *learn*, that is, obtain formal, conscious linguistic knowledge of rules of the second language" ("Planned Discourse" 175). By the term *acquisition*, Krashen means internalization of language rules as carried out by children, unconsciously, systematically, and without direct teaching. By contrast, *learning* is the process of internalizing rules through conscious effort and as a result of formal instruction. Krashen states that adult second language learners use both acquisition and learning; adult basic writers do likewise. Moreover, learned information functions in a special way as a monitor or editor of production from the acquired system.

The distinction between acquisition and learning invites a different perspective on errors. Krashen points out that, in the case of the third-person-singular -s marker among adult students of English as a second language (ESL), "many ESL performers have *learned* this item but have not *acquired* it—this is revealed in their variable performance—they get it right when they have time and are thinking about it, but may miss it otherwise" ("Planned Discourse" 176–77).

Error analysis in second language acquisition research comprises a whole subarea of second language research. This work had its beginnings in a now classic distinction by S. Pit Corder, a British linguist. In an early paper, Corder called attention to the systematic quality of learners' errors and their difference from mistakes. The distinction is summarized clearly by S. N. Sridhar, who maintains that "mistakes are deviations due to *performance* factors such as memory limitations . . . spelling pronunciations, fatigue, emotional strain, etc. They are typically random and are readily corrected by the learner when his attention is drawn to them. Errors, on the other hand, are systematic, consistent deviances characteristic of the learner's linguistic system at a given stage of learning" (105; see also Corder, "Significance"). Mistakes, then, are relatively chancy phenomena that are quite simple to deal with and that ought to yield to a few lessons in careful proofreading. Errors, more "resistant to instruction" (Shaughnessy ch. 4), must be viewed positively, as *good* signs of systematic attempts to master the redundancy of the system. The phrase "good errors" itself becomes redundant when errors are distinguished from mistakes.

In a later paper, Corder discussed these same issues in a different framework, calling the production of second language learners an "idiosyncratic dialect." These dialects, so named because they are rule-governed and share features with other languages, have many characteristics found in the production of basic writers: they follow rules peculiar to the individual alone; they are unstable; and individual sentences may be unclear. Errors, as composition teachers usually use the term, are merely manifestations of the learner's idiosyncratic dialect and are an "inevitable and indeed necessary part of the learning process" ("Idiosyncratic Dialects" 111). Idiosyncratic dialects occur among second language learners and among children, according to Corder, and they surely occur among basic writers as well.

Thus, among second language learners, as among children, the new language is acquired. Second language learners make errors in production, just as children do, usually as a result of the acquisition of a part or some parts of a complex system of rules, like those for past tense or agreement. Second language learners must internalize these rules and master their appropriate application to achieve proficiency. This process occurs in a staged fashion (called the "interlanguage" stage as discussed in chapter 4) and is marked by the systematic errors.

Like adult language learners, basic writers are engaged in the mastery of a new system of language rules. They also internalize the various rules in stages, with an intermediate stage of mastery marked by errors. Thus the development of writing skills is more a matter of acquisition than learning. Basic writers can be encouraged to work through their period of "good" errors in order to master the standard written form. Teachers who can spot systematic errors like those of the student discussed below will be able to facilitate the acquisition process. Support for this pattern of development can also be found in Bartholomae's case study "The Study of Error."

By focusing on a basic writer engaged in mastering the redundant features of English syntax, we have a practical "Monday morning" framework with which to consider several theories of second language acquisition and their relevance to writing acquisition. The work of this writer during a ten-week course in remedial composition demonstrates that writing is an acquired ability that shares characteristics with first and second language acquisition, including errors and inconsistent progress toward proficiency. Insights from first and second language acquisition research ask basic writing teachers to view errors as a necessary aspect of writing acquisition. This basic writing student shows evidence of acquisition—including the variable performance, rule testing and errors—in his attempts to master subject-verb agreement in the third person present tense. My student may have *learned* the rules for agreement as we discussed them in class but because he had just begun to *acquire* the rules, did not show consistent agreement in his essays. The acquisition process was quite unconscious on his part but not less real because he was unaware of it. His papers show the acquisition taking place: he makes many errors, consistently applies the rules he has developed, and revises his rules at least once.

This student shares many characteristics with other basic writers. GW is a black male, age twenty-six, educated at Western High

School in Detroit. Before college, he served three years in the U.S. Army and was stationed in Illesheim, West Germany. In GW's class, I used Betty Rizzo's text *The Writers' Studio*, having the students do some of the grammatical exercises and using many of the topics she provided in the writing exercises, but not assigning the exercises themselves. The students also completed twenty-eight writing assignments (some just one paragraph) during the term, divided evenly between in-class and homework assignments. The goal of the course, which is graded on a pass-fail basis, is to enable students to write a three-hundred word essay, using standard English grammar and reasonable organization and development.

GW was placed in our pre-freshman composition course by his score of 350 on the CEEB English Placement test (a multiple-choice grammar and usage test) and his performance on an in-class placement essay given on the first day of the term. Here is the opening paragraph of GW's placement essay on the U.S. boycott of the Moscow Olympics:

> I do not believe that the U.S. should send it's team to Moscow. The United States has allways been the first country to help others at any cost, and of course it's part of the human rights struggle to help those who need a helping hand. Russia, ever since 1954 when they attacked Checozavakia, who was no match for them defensively, and went on to construct a more than two mile blockade to keep the East Germans from going to the west, the *Russians* with their war machine, the red army, with their Mig 21 and 27 jet fighters and T52, and T54 battle tanks, by force *has* oppressed Eastern European Countries for decades. (Error in agreement italicized)

GW has made one agreement error here; this is his only agreement problem not only in this essay but in his first five papers. Moreover, the agreement difficulty may have resulted from the length and complexity of the sentence more than from the student's misunderstanding of the agreement rule that applies. Needless to say, he has a good many other problems. The papers presented below are a small sample of GW's work during the term, and although he makes many errors, his work with subject-verb agreement makes clear his systematic attempt to acquire the standard agreement rule.

The Writers' Studio encourages students to focus on subject-verb agreement. Of the thirty-six units in the book, six are devoted to various aspects of agreement. In GW's papers, his inability to be consistent about agreement seemed to surface in response to discussion of agreement in class. Here is a one paragraph paper GW wrote shortly before one of the early units on agreement:

> I was about fourteen years old. And on a Saturday, in May I was robbed. Ever since I have been very careful about, carrying large sums of money on me. I believe, that security is very important. I do not carry Money on me any more. Also I feel, that a person invites trouble, when he or she is carrying Money on them. This is a lesson I will never forget. (paper 13)

As soon as class discussion provided rules of agreement, GW began to make some errors. Two papers later, in the space of two paragraphs, he made four errors:

> I believe Students Should work, while they are in College. The Cost of education is rising and more students realize that having a job provides Security. A Student must schedule his time on the job and be able to attend his classes. A *student make* ends meet by working either full or part time. By working full or part time, the Student has the money to buy the merchandise *he need* and to keep up with the Cost of Education.
> The reason I believe Students should work while, in College is because the Cost of Education is rising. Also a Student must pay for the text book he uses. If a *Student work*, he can pay his tuition on time, if his Grants are not processed. I believe, if a *Student work* there Should be times put aside, so that the Student is not Complicating the Situation. Now a days, a Student must earn a Living for himself and at the same time educate himself. A working Student has more Control over his time. (paper 15)

Skeptical readers might argue that paper 13 is predominantly in first person and paper 15 is predominantly in third person and that it is only in third-person-singular present tense that agreement errors occur. However, the placement essay and the dependent clauses in paper 13 show that GW has some rules for agreement in both first and third person. Note that the four errors in paper 15 are all of one type, suggesting a rule that states "if the subject has no -s, do not put -s on the verb." This is indeed the standard rule for all verb forms except the third person singular of regular verbs, irregular verbs, and modals, but GW incorrectly extends it to the third person singular of regular verbs as well. He is off to a good start.

Three papers later, GW writes an essay mostly in the third person and shows that he has begun to realize that there are exceptions to his rule, leaving only two errors in about the same amount of text:

> I do believe Bad Experiences make people bitter. Because if a person gets up in the morning and finds out that, the clock is'nt working and he or she is late, that will provoke a bitter attitude, when the *person go* to work. I believe everyone now an then has good or bad days. We often attribute Bad Days, as the start of a bitter attitude. When a person has a bad experience, and is bitter, usually, everyone around can sense it. I also believe that if we do have Bad experiences we should try and Control our feelings.
>
> People become bitter, sometimes, when guilt *feelings is* felt. Bitterness and Bad Experiences go together. Sometimes I run into Bad situations, and I begin to feel bitter. If everyone could control their feelings we would'nt have bitterness. I have'nt seen an individual who could control all their emotions. I also believe, that Bad Experiences spark bitterness in everyone. (paper 18)

Of the two errors that occur here, only one results from the application of the rule GW formulated above. He has clearly begun to move toward the standard rule. The second error ("feelings is") is the first evidence of a revised rule for exceptions that emerges later. The inconsistency in the rule application results from the fact that GW has not acquired all aspects of the agreement rules.

GW's next three papers show no agreement errors whatsoever. Paper 22, however, shows twelve agreement errors and was written after another discussion of subject-verb agreement in class. These errors show a distinctive pattern, suggesting the GW has expanded his rule about the -s ending we use as the agreement marker.

> A student must choose his classes, by the degree requirements he must meet. The *student choose classes*, that *brings* him closer to his goal. Classes are chosen by the needs of the student. The *student choose* classes that are offered, at certain times of the day. Classes are chosen by

the student, if the *class offer* a certain subject. The student desides on the classes, that offer the best program.

A student looks for the best schedule he can get. A *student* most of the time *look* for a three day schedule. A student is more than likely going to pick a schedule that fits his needs. A student hopes that the classes he wants are still available to him during registration. A student must decide if his *program cover* the requirement *he need*. The *classes* a *student take depends* on want and need of the student.

The average student looks for classes, that will satisfy his degree requirements. The student looks for his classes during registration. The *student choose classes*, that *fills* his want and needs. The *student get* classes that he can plan his day around. The student must deside on the legnth of the class. The student must also deside on the amount of classes he will take. (paper 22)

The rule seems to be "put -s on if there's an -s on the subject, and leave it off if there's no -s on the subject." Note again the inconsistencies: GW uses the standard rule at the end of the first paragraph, for example, but in other places he is still trying his own revised rule.

The instability of GW's system is not really surprising in light of what is known about the interlanguage stage in which "good" errors appear during second language acquisition. This stage is marked by instability in the learner's production, just as Krashen has pointed out. We can speculate that GW may have *learned* some aspects of the agreement rule but not *acquired* all of them. The rules he has learned are applied inconsistently, quite in keeping with Krashen's claim that learned information is used only as a monitor on production, and then only under certain circumstances.

The differences between acquisition and learning account for some of the inconsistencies of basic writers, who seem to learn and forget the rules regularly and get subjects and verbs to agree occasionally because of good or poor proofreading, even after a period of seeming mastery. During the error period in basic writing (if we can apply the results of second language acquisition research), the learners' system is not stable and will show variable and often inconsistent patterns. Error analysis shows that this frustrating inconsistency is characteristic of acquisition in progress and must therefore be hailed as evidence of learners' success, not their failure or inability. GW's ultimate success (illustrated below) with the rules for agreement provides persuasive documentation that, despite inconsistencies, acquisition is taking place.

Paper 22 marks a middle point in GW's mastery of the rules for agreement in writing. He has begun to place the -s marker appropriately in the singular and to omit it in the plural, but his acquisition is still incomplete. This point is quite similar to the intermediate stage in children's acquisition of the past tense (tooked) and to a stage reached by second language learners in the interlanguage period. If GW's agreement errors reflect a rule-governed stage like that in second language acquisition (that is, interlanguage), then it is reasonable to expect increasing evidence of progress toward acquisition of the standard rule.

The next paper shows this expected development: GW's revised rule persists, but to a lesser extent, and it is clear that he has moved one step closer to consistent application of the standard rule.

> My Friend acts like two different people. My *friend attend* a college, and *he play* guitar. He is always playing the guitar. my friend plays guitar, more than he dose studying his school work. My friend has two personalities. He is always joking around.
>
> Some people act the same but not my friend, he has two personalities. My friend is a musician and a hard working student. My friend never acts like he's better than everyone. *He* always *find* time to do his homework from school. My friend is a good guitar player, and a had working student. My friend is a dedicated musician. (paper 23)

And three papers later, GW makes just one error in agreement, an error which, in Corder's terms, may very well be a mistake resulting from poor proofreading:

> The comparison between the White Shadow show, with the Tim Conway show. The White shadow is about a high school basketball team. Tim Conway Show is a Comedy show. The two are dealing with two different aspects of life,—comedy, and everyday life in high school. The comedy make's me laugh, and the high school setting makes me think of my old days in high school. The two pictures really do not compare in reality.
>
> I enjoy watching *pictures*, that *is* relavent. I watch picture's I can relate to. Both the White Shadow, and the tim conway show, have an interest in

audience understanding. I like pictures, that make me think, about to-day's world. The White shadow remids me, of the times I used to have in high school. Both picture's have a meaning behind the setting's. (paper 26)

This paper was written quite close to the end of the term. It is no masterpiece, but it does show that GW has acquired most aspects of standard subject-verb agreement.

I might have been quite depressed by GW's errors in paper 22, had I not seen the pattern operating in his writing. He had not failed to learn about agreement, nor did he lack a sense of the differ-ence between singular and plural. Instead, it seems clear that his rules, as he acquired them, were applied differently from the ones used in standard writing. The inconsistency in the application of the rules in paper 22 suggests that GW knew, even as he tested his ac-quired rules, that they were not quite right. Additional writing as-signments gave him a chance to test further and to revise, ultimately bringing his usage in line with the standard agreement rules.

GW's case shows that errors made by basic writers are "good" er-rors in that they are indicative of the students' perception of the re-dundancy of language and of writing as a rule-governed process. GW was not stupid or incapable of *learning* the rules: he simply needed adequate time and feedback to *acquire* all aspects of the subject-verb agreement system. GW's work has two messages for teachers of basic writing. First, look at the errors as errors, rather than mistakes, to see if there is a pattern to them. The pattern may be different from some aspects of the standard, as in GW's case, but errors, if they are systematic, are evidence of acquisition.

Not every error will conform to a pattern, but evidence from first and second language acquisition suggests that much language learn-ing activity, including learning to write, will show the patterned er-rors that come from the learner's efforts to acquire the redundancy of language. The pattern in errors is not always easy to see, and the writer's strategies will not always be easy to formulate. In second language acquisition or in writing acquisition, errors cannot yet be distinguished clearly from mistakes. However, teachers can watch for errors of a type recently discussed in class. Large numbers of a single type of error (like the twelve in GW's paper 22), particularly involving a redundant feature of language (like the agreement marker), may also be a diagnostic key. It might be reasonable to ask students to analyze their errors and make conscious their unconsciously acquired knowledge. Teachers must believe that students do acquire rules through hypothesis testing—GW's case documents the process in operation and shows that certain errors, notably those involving redundancy, are signs of "good" progress in writing acquisition.

The second message from GW's work is an old refrain that warrants repeating one more time: student writers must test their acquired knowledge in writing. Students must do a lot of writing to develop a sense of the special redundancy of written language, to observe their rules in operation, and to revise their rules until they approximate those of the standard written form. Given this opportunity, GW's work suggests that acquisition through systematic rule formation and testing creates the "good" errors by which basic writers achieve proficiency.

The analysis of errors in second language acquisition clarifies, in GW's case, the nature of his progress toward writing acquisition. The examination of error, generally, in chapters 4 and 5 supports the major hypothesis proposed here. GW's case also supports the second and third corollary hypotheses, concerning acquisition and learning and the ordering of acquisition processes. The fourth corollary, on the use of the monitor, is supported by GW's case and other cases reported in the literature (for example, by Bartholomae). The two final corollaries, on input and affective factors, can now be discussed in detail.

6

Affective Factors:
Pidginization in Basic Writing

PART OF UNDERSTANDING BASIC WRITERS' PROBLEMS REQUIRES AN understanding of their backgrounds. When basic writing students attempt to use the language of academia, they exhibit many of the same characteristics as do true second language learners. One these characteristics, which has been studied for second language learners, is pidginization. A pidginized language form is a simple cross between two or more languages, used for expedient communication. Unlike an interlanguage, which is a phenomenon unique to language learners, a pidgin may occur any time speakers of two different languages need to communicate with each other. John Schumann's research on pidginization in unsuccessful second language acquisition suggests that second language learners develop a pidginized language form as a result of their social and psychological distance from speakers of the target language (*Pidginization Process*). This pidginized form can be characterized by reduced redundancy and limited communication of information. Basic writers may have similar problems in writing as a result of their social and psychological distance from users of standard written language who are members of the academic establishment.

The distance between basic writers and members of the academic establishment has been described before. Relative to the academic community, basic writers are described by Mina Shaughnessy as

> the true outsiders. Natives, for the most part, of New York, graduates of
> the same public school system as the other students, they were nonethe-

less strangers in academia, unacquainted with the rules and rituals of college life, unprepared for the sorts of tasks their teachers were about to assign them. Most of them had grown up in one of New York's ethnic or racial enclaves. Many had spoken other languages or dialects at home and never successfully reconciled the worlds of home and school, a fact which by now had worked its way deep into their feelings about school and about themselves as students. (2–3)

These students are in alien territory in college: it is, for them, a foreign land with a foreign language and foreign customs. This sense of separateness on the part of basic writers contributes to social and psychological distance and that, in turn, contributes to the development of pidginized language forms.

Schumann's research on Alberto, a Costa Rican immigrant who was unsuccessful at mastering English as a second language, reveals many pidginization features in his language. No claim is made that Alberto uses a pidgin, only that his language forms show evidence of pidginization processes. Basic writers may show pidginization processes as well. Schumann's work suggests more strongly, however, that basic writing students' writing problems are the result of their social and psychological distance from users of the academic "target language." A comparison between Schumann's findings with Alberto and other second language students and the work of basic writers reveals many similarities and may be used to develop methods to enhance writing acquisition.

The original research project that led Schumann to examine Alberto's difficulties in acquiring a second language was carried out in 1973 in conjunction with several other researchers (*Pidginization Process*). The study involved a long-term examination of the acquisition of English by native speakers of Spanish who were not exposed to direct teaching. Six subjects were in the study: two children, two teenagers, and two adults (Alberto, age thirty-three, was one of the adult subjects).

In the ten-month longitudinal study, Alberto showed remarkably little linguistic development. Among Alberto's many problems with spoken English are: the negative form is not comparable to that used by a native speaker; in questions, Alberto usually fails to invert; and he has acquired relatively few auxiliary verb forms. Even more striking are the following features: the possessive tends to be unmarked in Alberto's speech; the regular past tense ending -ed is absent, and the progressive -ing appears only approximately 60 percent of the time (*Pidginization Process* 65–66). Note that these pidginized forms involve elements that are often syntactically redundant. Alberto's linguistic development in English was clearly limited compared to the development observed with other subjects in the study.

Schumann examines three possible factors in Alberto's lack of success in English: ability, age, and social and psychological distance. To eliminate the possibility that Alberto's trouble may have resulted from problems with cognitive or intellectual ability, all of the subjects were tested for cognitive ability (*Pidginization Process* 67–68). Based on this test, Alberto had no gross deficits that would preclude second language acquisition. A second possible cause for Alberto's failure to learn English was thought to be his age: thirty-three. In the literature in first and second language acquisition, there are a number of discussions of a proposed "critical period" for language acquisition (see Curtiss, deVilliers and deVilliers, and R. Brown). Those who support the critical-period hypothesis claim that language acquisition is a biological phenomenon that can only occur during a certain critical period, thought to be from birth to either age two or five or until puberty. The evidence in support of a biological critical period is weak at best and does not support the possibility that Alberto's age caused his difficulties in learning English (*Pidginization Process* ch. 8). However, an argument for a critical period tied not to biology but to cognitive or social development suggests that the learner must acquire language before reaching Piaget's stage of formal operations. Alberto was judged to be nearing formal operations on the basis of cognitive testing. Thus, neither biological nor cognitive development can account adequately for Alberto's problems. However, the argument for the possibility of a social critical period, a period tied to psychological and/or social development, is stronger. This argument suggests that second language difficulties occur *after* puberty because of social and psychological changes that occur *during* puberty, creating a distance between the second language learner and others. While Alberto's age in and of itself is not sufficient to account for his problems in learning English, age-related affective factors might account for problems he had during the time of the study.

Schumann explains that second language learners will show elements of pidginization as a result of their social and psychological distance from speakers of the second language. And he claims that early second language acquisition is a manifestation of the pidginization process ("Simplification"). The pidginization hypothesis is quite simple insofar as it claims that second language learners produce pidginlike forms; however, the hypothesis is based, first, on a line of analysis concerning pidgin languages and, second, on a line of analysis concerning social and psychological distance between the learner and the speakers of the target language. Each of these factors is also relevant to basic writers and to their problems in learning formal written English.

Schumann's proposals have been supported by extensive recent research into pidginization as a process. For example, Meisel, working in West Germany, reports the results of a study of forty-five adults learning German as a second language. The subjects of this study were foreign workers, a group of immigrants to Germany who preserved their separate identities as Italian or Spanish natives. His findings show clearly that "social-psychological factors influence natural second language acquisition in important ways. . . . [Moreover] . . . there is good evidence . . . that the kind of interlanguage variety a learner uses within one stage of an ordered sequence of developmental stages does, in fact, depend on the social setting and on resulting attitudes and motivation. Even if the relation between social-psychological and linguistic facts is not one of cause and effect, it is far from being arbitrary" (Meisel 153–54). Roger Andersen, whose work on second language acquisition has already been mentioned, presents his own view of language acquisition in his introduction to his edited collection *Pidginization and Creolization as Language Acquisition*. Andersen's research supports all of Schumann's findings and draws on a great deal of additional work that has been done ("Introduction" 1–56). Finally, Henning Wode's study is particularly relevant, both because it supports Schumann's work and the claims made here about the importance of pidginization in basic writing and because it represents Wode's attempt to unify various aspects of language acquisition into a single, comprehensive, integrated, unified theory of language acquisition. In this way, Wode's work moves in the same direction as the arguments presented in this book, as both contribute to the goal of discovering universal regularities in language acquisition. In his discussion of pidgins and creoles, Wode generally agrees with Schumann, and notes that "acculturation, social integration, i.e. affective variables of various sorts, affect progress. Despite some controversy over minor points there seems to be agreement now that pidginization is parallel to early L2 [second language] acquisition, and the decreolization is similar to later stages of L2 acquisition" (Wode 74). In basic writing research, evidence in support of the significance of affective factors comes from a study of 320 placement essays by Andrea Lunsford. Lunsford's work, comparing basic writers to those more skilled, shows clearly that such factors influence the content of basic writers' essays in important ways. Though some may question Lunsford's assumptions, my own contact with basic writers and many other students engaged in language skill development supports her analysis. Lunsford writes that "much evidence now points to the connection between poorly developed writing skills and poor self-image, lack of confidence, and lower levels of cognitive development" (284). Schumann, then, is not the only one to propose the pidginization hypothesis, and there is considerable support for his findings. His views are generally the most fully articulated statement of the influence of pidginization and thus serve as the basis for the discussion that follows.

Pidgin language forms occupy a central role in the discussion of various aspects of language acquisition. However, despite the research, no consensus exists about a definition of what precisely constitutes a pidgin language form. Schumann defines a pidgin as a "simplified and reduced form of speech used for communication between people with different languages" (*Pidginization Process* 69). Generally, pidgin language forms come about when speakers of two different languages are thrown together and have some urgent need to communicate with each other. Pidgins have no native speakers, generally develop as a matter of expediency, and are not full language forms. Schumann compares Alberto's English to the features of some well-established pidgin languages and finds many similarities in the linguistic features (*Pidginization Process* 70–71).

Let us turn to the basic writer. Even though the basic writer speaks standard English, the language that is used in academia, the basic writer might be described as dealing with a somewhat new language form. If we consider the basic writer as a stranger to academic language, then the basic writer's situation is very much like Alberto's. The basic writer's writing reflects the effects of social and psychological distance in the same way Alberto's language does.

What causes a pidgin to form? One of the more interesting responses is that the pidgin forms as a result of a restriction in language function. In this context, Schumann cites the work of David Smith:

> Smith ("Some Implications for the Social Status of Pidgin Languages," in *Sociolinguistics in Cross-Cultural Analysis*, ed. David M. Smith and Roger W. Shuy [Washington, D.C.: Georgetown University Press], 1972) sees language as having three general functions: communicative, integrative and expressive. The communicative function operates in the transmission of referential, denotative information between persons. The integrative function is engaged when a speaker acquires language to the extent that it marks him as a member of a particular social group. The expressive function goes beyond the integrative in that through it, the speaker becomes a valued member of a particular linguistic group. (*Pidginization Process* 76)

Pidgins are generally restricted to the communicative function. Similarly, the second language learner is restricted to the communicative function of language, at least in the early stages of acquisition. James Britton discusses the limited function of the basic writer's language and suggests that a similar situation applies in basic writing. In his discussion of the functions of writing, Britton lists three, on a continuous scale: the transactional function—to carry out operations of the intellect, to inform, to instruct, or to persuade; the expressive function—a loosely structured informal type of language used either to get things done or to evaluate experiences; and the poetic function—in which language becomes an end in and of itself (Britton 13–28). Although Britton's research shows relatively little expressive writing, I contend that basic writers begin with the expressive function in mind. This limitation of function is similar to that proposed by Smith. The communicative function used by speakers of a pidgin is similar to the expressive function described by Britton. As basic writers learn to carry out the transactional and poetic functions of language they move away from the restricted expressive or communicative function of language. Just as there are later stages in the development of a pidgin, so, too, are there later stages in the development of basic writers. Britton's expressive function and Smith's communicative function share in the urgent need to communicate information back and forth between people and in a relatively loose and simplified structure. In both cases, the restriction in function is a result of the social and psychological distance between the pidgin speaker or the basic writer and his or her audience.

The issue of distance is the remaining major claim of Schumann's pidginization hypothesis. According to Schumann, social distance and psychological distance promote pidginization among second language learners. Social distance deals with the interaction between two groups of speakers—those who already speak the language under study and those who are trying to learn it. The social factors that tend to promote or discourage interaction between these two groups have to do with the following set of factors: the dominance of the two groups in relation to each other, the integration pattern of the learner group, the degree of enclosure of the learner group, the cohesiveness of the learner group, its size, the congruence of the cultures of the speakers and learners, the attitudes of the two groups, and the duration of the learners' stay in the speakers' area. In thinking about the learner group, consider the situation of both the second language learner and the basic writer.

First, there is the question of dominance. The dominance of one group over another may be political, cultural, educational, or economic. If the speaker group is dominant in any one or more of these areas, social distance will separate the two groups. In the context of basic writers, professors and other members of the academic establishment are dominant with regard to level of education. For many basic writers, the superiority of their professors in terms of education alone is sufficient to create enormous social distance. Lunsford's study reports other ways in which basic writers feel separated from and oppressed by some aspects of society.

With regard to integration, the issue is whether the learner group seeks to assimilate, to acculturate, or to preserve its individual status. Do the learners want to give up their individuality and become like the speakers, do they want to adopt certain characteristics of the speakers but also maintain their individuality, or do they simply want to preserve their individual style and take on none of the characteristics of the speaker group? Schumann notes that "assimilation fosters minimal social distance and preservation causes it to be maximal. Hence second language learning is enhanced by assimilation and hindered by preservation. Acculturation falls in the middle" (*Pidginization Process* 78). For different basic writers, the goal in terms of integration will be necessarily different. Probably, those students who are intent on preservation will have the greatest difficulty in mastering the standard written form.

Enclosure and cohesiveness influence social distance as well. Both have to do with the closeness of the learner group and the associations among its members as distinct from its relationship to the speakers' group. The point at issue is how much contact is likely to occur between the speakers and the learners. Thus, if the learners tend to be in the same schools, churches, and recreational facilities as the speakers, they are said to have low enclosure, whereas if the contact between the two groups is minimal, the enclosure is high. Similarly, cohesiveness is a matter of contact between the two groups, highly dependent upon the size of each group. Clearly, less enclosure and less cohesiveness in the learner group lowers the social distance between the learners and the speakers.

Alberto was part of a group that was highly enclosed and highly cohesive, hence his pidginized language and lack of success. Basic writers may or may not be part of a highly enclosed and cohesive group. Again, the situation varies considerably with the individuals involved. In a certain sense, however, the members of the academic establishment tend to be a highly enclosed and highly cohesive group. It is reasonable, therefore, to assume that considerable social distance exists between basic writers and the academic establishment.

Congruence and attitude also affect social distance. The congruence of two groups has to do with the extent to which they are similar culturally, and the attitudes of the speakers and learners are often a byproduct of this cultural congruence. If the speakers and learners are culturally similar and view one another positively, the social distance will be reduced. If, on the other hand, the two groups are quite different and have negative expectations, the social distance will be enhanced. These factors, like the others that affect social distance, have been studied to some degree for second language learners but not for basic writers. Social distance may well be an important factor in the acquisition of writing skills.

Finally, Schumann considers the length of stay—how long will the learner be in the speaker's area—a factor that seems to apply almost exclusively to second language learners. However, if one considers the basic writer's frequent expectation that he or she will be upwardly mobile as the result of a college education and its attendant mastery of formal written language, then this factor applies equally to second language learners and basic writers. The basic writer often hopes to spend the rest of his or her life, if not in the academic establishment, then at least in areas in which members of the academic establishment are likely to be respected and comfortable. Schumann contends that a lengthy stay in the speakers' area will tend to reduce social distance (*Pidginization Process* 80). Ideally, the social distance between basic writers and members of the academic establishment would be similarly reduced, but more likely the other factors contributing to social distance between basic writers and their teachers would override this length of stay factor.

Social distance, then, restricts the language of speakers to a communicative function level, and the restriction in function is manifested by pidginization. Alberto's English production shows considerable evidence of pidginization, which probably results from his social distance from English speakers. Similarly, a significant social distance between basic writers and speakers of their "target language" (formal written English) results in writing problems. For basic writers, distance factors inhibit development of a sense of redundancy of language, and pidginized forms concentrate on those syntactically redundant elements.

In addition to restricted function and social distance, the existence of psychological distance between the learner and the speaker also contributes to the formation of a pidginlike language. Psychological distance is defined by a group of factors that affect an individual and that may override social distance factors inhibiting language learning. Schumann gives a reasonably precise definition of his concept of psychological distance by saying that "an individual might learn the target language where he is expected not to, and not learn the language where successful acquisition is expected. In these cases it is *psychological* distance or proximity between the learner

and the TL [target language] group that accounts for successful versus unsuccessful second language acquisition" (*Pidginization Process*
86). Psychological distance is composed of language and culture
shock, motivation, and ego permeability. Each of these factors will
also turn out to be relevant to the basic writing student.

According to Schumann, language and culture shock are the primary factors that create psychological distance. Both concern the
way individuals relate to people around them. In the case of language shock, the problem is whether individuals can convey the
ideas they have in mind in their new language. Failure to convey the
intended meaning can create a great deal of anxiety and frustration
for the individual. In the case of culture shock, the standard mechanisms an individual has developed to cope with everyday life fail to
work in the new culture. The result is anxiety and frustration.

The language and culture shock problem is useful in accounting
for Alberto's failure to learn English. It can also be extended to the
problems of basic writers. As aliens to academic language and academic culture, basic writers experience language and culture shock
in the basic writing classroom, sometimes in all their classes. As language learning is inhibited by psychological distance, basic writers
must be helped to make a language and culture adjustment if they
are to master the new language form. The need for assistance in
making this adjustment is as pressing for basic writers trying to learn
formal written English as it is for immigrants or other second language learners trying to adjust to a new situation.

Motivation is another element that contributes to psychological
distance. Motivation has been studied extensively in the context of
second language learning (Gardner and Lambert). A now classic distinction is made between integrative motivation and instrumental
motivation. Schumann discusses this distinction in some detail. "An
integratively-oriented learner is interested in acquiring the second
language in order to meet and communicate with valued members of
the target language community. A learner with an instrumental ori-
entation is one who has little interest in the people who speak the
target language, but nevertheless wants to learn the language for
more self-oriented or utilitarian reasons, such as getting ahead in his
occupation or gaining recognition from his own membership group"
(*Pidginization Process* 91). Clearly, the learner with the integrative
motivation has less of a problem with psychological distance than

does the learner with instrumental motivation. Alberto's instrumental motivation contributed to his psychological distance from speakers of English and therefore to his difficulties in mastering the language.

The distinction between integrative and instrumental motivation applies to basic writers as well. Shaughnessy discusses the distinction and its application to basic writers and points out that it is extremely difficult for basic writing students to develop any integrative motivation with regard to the mastery of formal written English:

> When we remember the ways in which the majority society has impinged upon the lives of most BW students and when we recall the students' distrust of teachers and their language, engendered over years of schooling, it is difficult to see how the desire to identify with the majority culture, and therefore its public language, could possibly have survived into young adulthood. At best we might expect deeply ambivalent feelings about "making it" in a course that teaches what is perceived as an alien dialect. Even the instrumental motive is likely to be weak among students who are not yet in the habit of seeing themselves in careers. (125)

In regard to motivation, basic writing students are likely to have a maximum amount of psychological distance from the academic language they are trying to learn. This distance inhibits mastery of redundancy and other elements of the formal writing system.

Schumann's third contributor to psychological distance among language learners is ego permeability. Ego permeability is linked closely to the psychological construct of a language ego such as that proposed by Alexander Guiora. Language ego is developed in tandem with the body ego or general ego as described by Freud. Schumann explains Guiora's idea as follows: "Guiora sees language ego as the development of language boundaries. In the course of general ego development, the lexis, syntax, morphology and phonology of the individual's language acquire physical outlines and firm boundaries. In the early formative stages of ego development the language barriers fluctuate but once ego development is completed, the permeability of the boundaries is sharply restricted" (*Pidginization Process* 94). Guiora's studies suggest evidence of language ego and its relative permeability, but there is no firm evidence to establish this concept. Guiora's research does show, however, that it is possible to induce greater permeability of ego boundaries in adults. This fact, in turn, suggests that if the permeability of ego boundaries is an important factor in language acquisition, then our ability to increase permeability will enhance learning.

Although there are weaknesses in the research on ego permeability, the notion of psychological distance has appeal because it encourages us to examine each student as part of a larger social group that may inhibit or enhance language learning and also as an individual with psychological and personality characteristics that may enhance and/or inhibit language learning. In this way, Schumann's discussion of social and psychological factors provides a radically different way of looking at the language learner. Both second language learners and those in the process of acquiring formal written English are clearly affected by elements of both social and psychological distance, which impede linguistic progress. They do so partly because distance limits learners' opportunities to develop a sense of the redundancy of language.

The characteristics of Alberto's language that are parallel to those found in true pidgin languages are also similar to those found in the work of basic writers. Many of the elements mentioned as features of Alberto's linguistic development in English may also apply to basic writers; these elements are often syntactically redundant features like problems with negation, difficulty in forming questions appropriately, problems with the possessive marker, the instability of the past tense -ed, and the progressive -ing forms. These characteristics are documented extensively in the work of Shaughnessy and others (Shaughnessy ch. 4 and her sources). Keep in mind that Schumann does not claim that Alberto spoke a pidgin, nor does basic writing qualify as a pidgin language form. Rather, basic writers' problems can be accounted for in part by the same social and psychological factors that produced pidginized forms in Alberto's speech.

A 1985 study of creole features in the work of basic writers provides detailed evidence to support the discussion of this chapter. A creole form of a language is "a language which has a pidgin in its ancestry. . . . Children . . . who heard no other language but the pidgin made it their mother tongue, creating the creoles that became established as the language of the community" (Holm 2). Creoles are marked by expansion of pidgin vocabulary and grammatical structure, but they are still different from the standard languages which are their source. That is, creoles can be described as a more complex and fully developed form of a pidgin. Thus, the findings of a study of creole features in the work of basic writers supports the general argument of this chapter.

John Holm found some twenty linguistic problem features in the work of basic writers taking composition at Hunter College in New York City. The features include subject-verb agreement problems, lack of the -ed marker on verbs, variations in the form of *to be*, and a variety of noun phrase, verb phrase and word order features found in the creole languages spoken by these students. From this evidence, there can be little doubt that pidgin and creole features appear in the work of basic writers, and the work of Schumann and others suggests that social and psychological distance factors are the chief reasons why these forms appear and persist in students' written work.

If we are going to understand what learners are doing and why they fail to learn, we must look in great detail at the affective factors that play a role in the acquisition of formal written English. These factors provide an important key to GW's writing problems and might, had I known how to overcome the distance problem, have helped me facilitate his progress. Schumann's pidginization hypothesis "predicts that where social and psychological distance prevail, we will find pidginization persisting in the speech of second language learners" (*Pidginization Process* 115). By extension, the pidginization hypothesis also predicts that basic writers affected by distance factors will have writing problems. The problem for teachers and researchers in basic writing is to understand the affective factors that contribute to a writing student's social and psychological distance. Ultimately, teachers must find ways to bridge the social and psychological distance between basic writers and those who use formal written English. John Schumann's careful research gives us a new set of materials with which to build such a bridge.

7

Monitor Theory

WE HAVE LOOKED AT TWO ANALYSES OF SECOND LANGUAGE AC-
quisition that account for learners' difficulties in mastering a new
language: error analysis and an analysis of affective factors. Both approaches are relevant to the acquisition of writing insofar as writing
is a distinct language and insofar as mastery of the written form
requires mastery of the specific redundancy of written language.
Stephen Krashen's monitor theory incorporates error analysis and
the role of affective factors into a third theory of second language
acquisition. The monitor theory's central hypothesis is that language
ability is developed through *acquisition* (unconscious, internal, and
systematic processes) and *learning* (conscious, explicit mastery of
rules). Learned information functions as a monitor on production
from the acquired system. Since writing ability, and particularly a
sense of the redundancy of written language, must also be acquired
and learned, monitor theory, when it is extended to writing acquisition, yields significant insights. Krashen has suggested ways in
which the theory can be applied to the acquisition of writing skills
("Planned Discourse"), and Ross Winterowd ("From Classroom
Practice") and Barbara Kroll have extended and expanded the monitor to aspects of teaching and learning writing.

In a presentation at the 1981 TESOL Convention, Krashen described the monitor theory in its broad outlines. In this presentation, Krashen outlined the five major hypotheses concerning the
mastery of a new language ("Consequences"). The first distinguishes
between acquisition and learning. Adult students of a second language may use one or the other or both of these strategies. Acquisition processes are those unconscious, systematic procedures

whereby learners set up and test personally constructed rules for the language. Adult second language students also make use of learning, which is the conscious and explicit strategy for language mastery which most teachers hope that students employ. The acquisition/learning distinction is central to monitor theory.

Krashen's second hypothesis is that the language learner masters elements through acquisition in an ordered fashion. This hypothesis derives from research in first language acquisition that examines the acquisition of certain key morphemes (minimal units of meaning, including words and meaningful word endings like the -s plural) in a child's acquisition of the first language. The phenomenon of natural ordering in acquisition for children and adults is quite well established in the research literature (R. Brown, Krashen "Monitor Model," and deVilliers and deVilliers). The existence of natural ordering, even though acquisition orders differ for first and second language, and the evidence of a natural acquisition order among adults support the distinction between acquisition and learning. Like the learning of a second language, writing is also acquired in a stagelike fashion.

The third hypothesis in the monitor theory, and the one for which the theory is named, is that those rules of language that are mastered through the conscious effort of learning function only as a monitor on the output of the acquired language system. This claim may be the most controversial element in the theory. Conscious learning is what teachers hope goes on in the classroom. As such, conscious learning involves explicit teaching; it involves the teaching of rules, and it seems to benefit from error correction. In further support of the distinction between acquisition and learning, the byproducts of conscious learning do not seem to show a natural ordering in the same way the byproducts of acquisition do. The essence of the monitor theory lies in the notion that learning functions only as an editor of what the learner produces based on acquisition. The monitor operates notably on the redundant elements in language, whether written or spoken.

Several important constraints on the use of the monitor by an individual exist: the learner must have time in which to cause the monitor to operate; the learner must be "focusing on form"; and the learner must have knowledge of the rules that apply in the particular situation in which the monitor comes into play. Krashen has written extensively on the amount of individual variation in the use of the monitor ("Some Issues," "Individual Variation"). Some people apparently make excellent use of the monitor, while others either overuse or underuse it. Before we can examine this claim about learning functioning as a monitor, it will be useful to look at the remainder of the hypotheses.

The fourth is the input hypothesis, which states that acquisition occurs when there is "comprehensible input" for the learner. Comprehensible input contains structures that are slightly beyond the capacity of the learner but nonetheless comprehensible, given the context in which they occur. Input must be deeply meaningful and varied, must occur in great quantity, and must lower the learner's psychological and/or social resistance to information. In his discussion of input, Krashen also introduces the term *intake*, borrowed from Corder, which "refers to that input that enables an acquirer to acquire more of a target language. It is a proper subset of input. Input may include a great deal of language that is of no help in the acquisition process" ("Monitor Model for Acquisition" 15). For input to become intake, it must be understood, be somewhat complex, and be provided in the context of interesting and natural communication. The classroom may be the best and often the only source of comprehensible input for adult learners. Thus, the teacher plays a crucial role in selecting or providing comprehensible input on which acquisition is based. Moreover, Krashen has recently discussed extensive evidence in support of the input hypothesis (Krashen et al., "Theoretical Basis" 270–73).

The fifth hypothesis in the monitor theory is the affective filter hypothesis, whereby affective factors filter input. The affective filter screens out even the most useful input if the learner's internal state is not conducive to acquisition taking place (if the learner is extremely anxious, for example). The provider of comprehensible input, then, must take note of the learner's affective filter, and comprehensible input must lower the learner's affective filter. The best input in the world will not be integrated by the adult learner unless the affective filter is "down."

Before going on to connect the monitor theory to the problems of teaching writing, we can integrate it with the theories discussed previously. The interlanguage hypothesis and the pidginization hypothesis both fit fairly well into the monitor theory. The interlanguage hypothesis complements Krashen's first and second hypotheses concerning the monitor (that is, acquisition and learning are two different strategies for mastering a language, and the process of acquisition shows a natural order). Drawn in part from first language acquisition evidence, these two hypotheses suggest that many adults master language in much the same way children do, and that there are clear stages that the learner moves through in order to achieve proficiency. Selinker's evidence suggests that the interlanguage stage is clear, and he and Krashen would surely agree on the fact that the interlanguage stage is one way of accounting for some of the behavior we find during language acquisition. Many of the phenomena that Selinker believes characterize the interlanguage stage are also found in the work of basic writers and children acquiring their native language.

The pidginization hypothesis relates to the affective filter hypothesis of the monitor theory. Schumann's work with Alberto and that of other researchers suggests that the role of affective factors is significant in language acquisition. The reason Alberto failed to master English as a second language successfully was that his social and psychological distance from speakers of English created certain pidginized forms in his English production, and he had no motivation to remove those pidginized forms. If social and psychological distance tend to inhibit language acquisition, then the affective filter apparently plays a key role in language acquisition. Thus, the advantage of the monitor theory is that it presents a fairly complete analysis of the entire process of second language acquisition, which has important implications for the teaching and learning of basic writing.

Krashen has seen the usefulness of the monitor theory for the teaching and learning of writing. He discussed the implications of this model in a paper entitled "On the Acquisition of Planned Discourse: Written English as a Second Dialect." He begins with the hypothesis that written English is a second language and that its acquisition is similar in many ways to the acquisition of a second language. Drawing on the work of Elinor Keenan, Krashen initially distinguishes among three levels or types of discourse: unplanned discourse found in spontaneous conversation, planned discourse that is informal written narrative and description, and well-planned discourse, or formal expository writing. Planned and well-planned discourse are different from unplanned discourse in that the unplanned is most commonly, but not exclusively, spoken whereas both planned and well-planned are usually written. Within the confines of written discourse, however, Krashen also finds distinctions in text characteristics ("Planned Discourse" 174). Krashen believes that the acquisition of both planned and well-planned discourse is like the acquisition of a second language.

Krashen also believes that the hypotheses that comprise the monitor theory are relevant to the acquisition of writing (*Writing* 21–24). In particular, the initial distinction between acquisition and learning and the claim that structures are acquired in order are applicable. Krashen gives a description of students of English as a second language (ESL) that might also be a description of the behavior of basic writers:

> An important commentary is that conscious monitoring can enable an adult to "outperform his acquired competence." For example, the third person singular morpheme is generally acquired relatively late. It is, however, fairly easy to conceptualize and learn and is taught early. Many ESL performers have *learned* this item but have not *acquired* it—this is revealed in their variable performance—they get it right when they have time and are thinking about it but may miss it otherwise. ("Planned Discourse" 177)

Many basic writers, like the one described in chapter five, show this "variable performance." If the monitor theory is correct, the explanation for variable performance comes from the distinction between acquisition and learning and from the fact that structures are acquired in some kind of order. Krashen, like Selinker, is claiming that there are clear stages in the acquisition of writing skills.

Krashen's third hypothesis, that learned material functions only as a monitor on the output of the acquired system, is strongly supported by David Bartholomae's research. Although Bartholomae's study reports results with only one basic writer, there is much other research in reading to suggest that Bartholomae's findings will hold across larger populations (Goodman and Goodman). Bartholomae found that when his basic writer read his writing aloud, he corrected a great many of the errors he made. That is, his monitor functioned well when he was focusing on form and had the time to make use of it. Bartholomae says that we can capitalize on this ability and help basic writers be more accurate by teaching them to use the monitor appropriately when they write.

Other researchers have attempted to help basic writers in just this way. For example, Douglas Adamson has compared the claims about the monitor made by Krashen to those made by Labov. Adamson believes that monitoring works in two ways. First, following Krashen, the monitor comes into play when the student makes conscious use of consciously learned rules. Second, as Labov has suggested, the monitor may also work unconsciously when the student edits with a "feel for correctness" (Adamson 6). Susan Dicker makes a similar suggestion in her discussion on teaching ESL writers. She suggests a twofold approach to editing that might be helpful to basic writers. Her strategy is to have the writer make two editing runs through the text, one for communicative accuracy and a second for grammatical accuracy. If the second pass makes use of the reading miscue approach advocated by Bartholomae, basic writers are likely to be much more successful in demonstrating their ability to produce formal written English. Dicker's plan would allow students to draw on both their learned and acquired ability with the special language of academia.

The fourth hypothesis from monitor theory that Krashen applies to composition is that comprehensible input is necessary for language acquisition to take place. Comprehensible input must contain understandable material a little bit beyond the acquirer's present level, be varied in content, be presented in large quantity, and reduce the affective filter. To be of use in acquisition, this input must occur in the context of natural language. Input that meets all the criteria set up by Krashen is likely to become intake, that is, material that the learner can actually use. It is also important to help students learn to write for truly communicative (albeit simulated) reasons. A similar goal of "communicative competence" also appears in the literature on second language acquisition (Rivers).

The final monitor hypothesis is the affective filter hypothesis, which states that acquisition is most likely to occur when the affective filter is lowered, that is, when the learners are receptive to intake. Krashen says that attitudinal factors exert significant control over language acquisition but have limited influence on learning. In contrast, aptitude or inherent ability is critical to learning, while attitudes play a lesser role. Insofar as writing is acquired, attitudinal and psychological factors play a central role and need much more attention from scholars. Since aptitude plays the overriding role in learning, it is possible for basic writers to learn some aspects of writing but not acquire them. Many basic writers have significant attitudinal barriers to the acquisition of formal expository writing, barriers that are largely ignored in the research literature.

The attitude factor captured by the affective-filter hypothesis may account for many difficulties of basic writers and in particular may help with error. Krashen takes up the problem of error in the context of a discussion about editing. He notes that editing may simply be a matter of taking elements of unplanned discourse (that is, conversational elements) out of planned discourse. The presence of unplanned discourse in the written or planned form could be a source of error in writing. The adult beginner may use the monitor to edit planned and well-planned discourse, and the monitor may make a distinction between the rules of spoken and written forms. Krashen has confined the monitor to its function based on conscious rules, but the monitor *may* function to separate unplanned from planned elements. Elements of unplanned discourse may appear in the written work of the basic writer, and basic writers might well profit from learning to distinguish between rules for spoken forms and rules for written forms. This approach has rarely been advocated in any basic writing text, although de Beaugrande's new one, *Writing Step by Step*, moves in this direction.

Despite the virtues of this approach, many problems lie in Krashen's claims concerning unplanned and planned discourse. First, the rules for planned discourse have not all been discovered and may not be presentable even when they have been discovered. Moreover, the distinctions between unplanned, planned, and well-planned discourse are not yet completely clear. In addition, Krashen notes that the stages a writer moves through need much study, requiring longitudinal investigation. Relatively few such studies have been begun. If Krashen is correct that informal, descriptive, and narrative writing is acquired during the public school years, while well-planned discourse is acquired at a later point, the research needed is much more "longitudinal" than is commonly thought. Despite these problems, however, monitor theory carries over to the situation of the basic writer and sheds much light on basic writers' problems.

Several further applications of the monitor to the teaching and learning of writing are also productive. For instance, Barbara Kroll amplifies the role of the monitor in the basic writer who may rely on both learning and acquisition to master the written form. In addition, Kroll extends the monitor to aspects of discourse in basic writing, with a distinction between acquisition and learning. Kroll points out, as Krashen does, that some students may acquire the written form of language and others may not. In general, the rules followed by writers who have acquired the written form are those that Kroll calls "morphosyntactic." Knowledge of the morphosyntactic rules can come about through learning or acquisition. "It is important to stress that such mastery can be conscious or unconscious, that is, mastery can stem from an acquired proficiency or a learned one. What does appear to be the case is that these sorts of features—the morphosyntactic 'rules'—lend themselves to rule isolation and can be taught to students to form part of the monitor for those people who lack an acquired mastery system" (Kroll 5–6). Thus, what some students will achieve through acquisition, others must achieve through learning, and Kroll points out that mastery may be achieved through either acquisition or learning.

Kroll also notes that, in addition to morphosyntactic rules, writers must achieve mastery over discourse-level principles. Kroll extends the monitor to these discourse level principles:

> Because discourse level principles are difficult to "chunk" and difficult to define, at this level a monitor of "grammaticality and appropriateness" (Krashen's terms) seems to have no role. I would like to suggest that a combination of conscious and unconscious knowledge combines to form a kind of discourse monitor, which is closely related to editing. My use of the term "monitor" here is meant to refer to a theoretical overseer which looks at the message and adjusts it appropriately without necessarily appealing to a specific "rule" to do so. (5–6)

Kroll's point is that the monitor, a body of consciously learned information and rules, need not be limited simply to morphosyntactic elements; it may also include the larger principles of organization, development, and coherence, which are also part of the nature of good writing.

One might wonder whether this extension of the monitor theory, or the monitor itself, to discourse level elements is legitimate. A review of the various levels of redundancy in language and of the crucial role of redundancy in communicating suggests that both Krashen's monitor (consciously learned rules for written forms or syntactic redundancy) and the discourse monitor (drawing on unconsciously acquired principles or semantic redundancy) play a key role in writing. If the byproducts of learning function only as a monitor, and if discourse principles can be learned through conscious effort, then these same discourse principles can function as part of the monitoring system. It may also be true, however, that discourse principles must be acquired, as must certain morphosyntactic principles. If this turns out to be the case, then discourse principles, although they may be learned, must also be acquired if they are to find their way into writers' production. Moreover, H. Douglas Brown suggests that acquisition and learning should be viewed as points on a continuum rather than as two mutually exclusive possibilities, in keeping with Kroll's discussion (Brown, "Consensus" 277).

W. Ross Winterowd makes precisely this point concerning the acquisition of discourse or rhetorical principles. According to Winterowd, certain aspects of rhetorical skill must be acquired, but he disagrees with Krashen on how this acquisition takes place. In the input hypothesis, Krashen states that, in order for acquisition to take place, there must be input that has specific characteristics. According to Winterowd, acquisition of writing ability comes through the input of reading, as Krashen has said; but Winterowd adds that feedback is also necessary (Winterowd, "Classroom Practice" 8–9). Rhetorical skills are *acquired*, in Winterowd's view, but depend on both input and feedback. Krashen's most recent view is that feedback may be valuable, but only in developing performance skills needed for the writing process.

Winterowd also proposes that mastery of certain aspects of writing comes about through neither learning nor acquisition. Instead, mastery may be achieved through "hands on" experience with language. This experience may derive from exercises like sentence combining, or in a writing workshop situation, or in some other feedback situation. Krashen's response to this would probably be that intensive active involvement sets a perfect stage for acquisition to take place. Nonetheless, Winterowd's view enriches the monitor theory by suggesting a role for rhetorical elements. The claim is simply that rhetorical elements are developed through both input, as suggested by Krashen, and feedback. Winterowd, then, proposes a revised monitor theory, "the result of experience and rhetorical theory," which may look like this:

> *Acquisition:* the "learning" of the skills of (rhetoric) through input and feedback.
>
> *Learning:* the "learning" of a-rhetorical skills through rules, algorithms, paradigms, and programmed exercises. ("Classroom Practice" 14)

Again, we have the suggestion that the monitor theory can be expanded in such a way as to incorporate discourse or rhetorical principles that are regarded as essential aspects of the written form.

The work of Kroll and of Winterowd might leave the impression that acquisition is everything in learning to write and that conscious learning, whether it produces a discourse-level monitor or not, has little value in the acquisition of writing and of second language skills. Krashen, however, discusses the benefits of conscious learning. Conscious learning may benefit those who have learned to use the monitor in an optimal way—those who seem to know when to apply the monitor and when to ignore it. Those optimal monitor users can improve their accuracy with the language as a result of conscious learning. In addition, conscious learning is relevant activity when one is teaching students *about* the language rather than teaching them the language, and, as Shaughnessy has pointed out, students are interested in such "linguistic data."

Finally, conscious learning may also help those who use the monitor too much (Pianko 5–22). Many basic writers who seem to edit as they produce written work may benefit from conscious learning because it can give them a kind of "faith" in the operation of the acquisition system. Many students distrust acquisition; when they have consciously learned something, they report that it confirms something they knew all along, that is, something they acquired. Thus, conscious learning is not without its advantages and may be particularly important for the adult beginner, either in second language acquisition or in basic writing. Moreover, many students want to be given "the rules" and enjoy linguistic analysis. A further point concerning conscious learning has to do with the interrelationship between the byproducts of acquisition and learning. For Krashen, the only role for material achieved through conscious learning is as a monitor on the output of the acquired system. This claim about the separation of learning and acquisition raises an interesting question with regard to basic writing. Perhaps the byproducts of learning and acquisition are not as separate for basic writers as they are for second language learners. The central role of redundancy in language and the particular redundancy of written language suggest this possibility. On the other hand, despite claims that the written form has a status as a distinct language, certain undeniable similarities are apparent between the spoken and written form of a language: words, certain grammatical patterns, discourse structures, and so on. Thus, in the mastery of written forms, perhaps the material that is learned and the material that is acquired interact more than they do in second language acquisition. Winterowd's suggestions imply this, and research on redundancy supports this view. If acquisition and learning interact in the basic writer, the teacher becomes much more critical, serving as a facilitator of acquisition and as a source of consciously learned material.

Teachers of basic writing, understanding the distinction between acquisition and learning and the interaction of the two systems, may be able to help students become optimal monitor users. Research in the composing process suggests that some students monitor too much (Perl 317–36). If the monitor is a byproduct of conscious learning, it is possible that *use* of the monitor could also be a byproduct of conscious learning. We may be able to teach students to rely on what they have acquired to produce a complete piece of text, and only then apply the monitor to it. The monitor, as Krashen describes it, particularly as enriched by Kroll and Winterowd, should allow students to tap both what they have acquired and what they have learned, in a reasonably efficient manner.

William Acton at the University of Houston has been working with native speakers of English and with second language learners, as he reported at the 1981 meeting of Teachers of English to Speakers of Other Languages (TESOL). His preliminary research suggests that it is possible to teach learners to apply the monitor under certain carefully specified sets of circumstances, while maintaining their fluency in the language. If Acton's "language acquisition heuristics" can be extended to the acquisition of writing skills, it may be possible to teach learners to make conscious use of the monitor in writing. The results of this research are still forthcoming.

Meanwhile, monitor theory has strong intuitive appeal in both second language acquisition and the teaching and learning of writing. The search continues for a model of the writing process and the writing product, in short, for a complete picture of writing ability. Nowhere is this need greater than among teachers and students of basic writing.

Krashen makes the claim in monitor theory that, while instruction appears to play a role in the mastery of language, acquisition actually proceeds more or less on its own—in the presence of comprehensible input, a low affective filter, and so on. Learning, meanwhile, is a byproduct of conscious effort and functions only as a monitor on the acquired system. Because research in second language acquisition is further along and more sophisticated than research in composition, basic writing teachers may be able to apply the findings of researchers in second language. Hopefully, despite important criticism of Krashen's work (McLaughlin and Munsell and Carr, and more recently Hammerly), research on the monitor will provide teachers and learners with a model.

The monitor, particularly when extended to discourse and rhetorical aspects of writing, accounts for what students know and what they do—for the acquisition and use of redundancy in writing. The input hypothesis, like other aspects of the monitor theory, has already been the subject of considerable debate and will require much additional study. The affective-filter hypothesis for second language learners, supported by the research of John Schumann, is the one which seems to have the most direct bearing on the situation of the basic writer, but it has been virtually ignored in the literature on writing. (Krashen points out that the affective filter relates to input, not writing performance, where much recent work has been centered. Thus, it is no surprise that affective matters have been ignored in basic writing theory.) In any event, monitor theory seems to tie in very closely to some things we already know about the teaching and learning of writing and has the potential to shed light on other areas in a profitable way. Monitor theory will surely require much expansion and modification in its development as a global model of second language acquisition and even more modification as a global model for basic writing. However, it is a model that has strong potential to achieve a level of explanatory adequacy (Chomsky, *Aspects* 27), a level much too rare in the work on basic writing.

Krashen and Schumann together support the last two hypotheses in the theory of writing acquisition—the input hypothesis and the affective filter hypothesis. The two are closely related because unless students can be persuaded to lower their filters, they cannot make use of input, no matter how good it is. Overall, then, second language studies show clearly how language abilities develop, and there is good reason to carry these principles over to the development of writing skills. The final chapter reviews these claims and those discussed earlier, as they provide an outline for further research in basic writing.

8

Conclusion

MANY WRITERS HAVE SPECIFIED THAT ANY MODEL OR THEORY
that has to do with language must be both simple and elegant, just
like other scientific theories and models. Noam Chomsky is one of
the writers who has dealt with models of language in a most com-
pelling discussion. Chomsky discusses the question of the scientific
elegance and simplicity of models in a chapter of *Rules and Representations*. Consider, for example, these comments by Chomsky on
the work of the immunologist Niels Kaj Jerne:

> He distinguishes between instructive and selective theories in biology,
> where an instructive theory holds that a signal from outside imparts its
> character to the system that receives it, and a selective theory holds that
> change of the system takes place when some already present character
> is identified and amplified by the intruding stimulus. He argues that
> "Looking back into the history of biology, it appears wherever a phenom-
> enon resembles learning, an instructive theory was first proposed to ac-
> count for the underlying mechanisms. In every case, this was later re-
> placed by a selective theory." The primary example that he deals with is
> the development of antibodies by the immune system. This was first as-
> sumed to be a kind of learning process in which the antigen played an
> instructive role, the reason being that the number of antigens was so im-
> mense, including even artificially synthesized substances that had never
> existed in the world, that no other account seemed conceivable. But this
> theory has been abandoned. An animal "cannot be stimulated to make
> specific antibodies, unless it has already made antibodies of this specific-
> ity before the antigen arrives," so that antibody formation is a selective

process in which the antigen plays a selective and amplifying role. (Chomsky, *Rules* 136–7)

We may need to exchange our "instructive theories," those that deal with teaching methodology and classroom practice, for selective theories like the monitor theory. If Chomsky is right in his long-standing contention that "grammar grows in the mind" (Chomsky, *Rules* 134), then language is in fact acquired much as Krashen contends in his monitor theory. According to Chomsky, no language can develop in the human being without some prior innate system that would predispose such production. Again, if Chomsky is right, Krashen's monitor theory and my extension of his view are a natural outgrowth of this claim. Just as scientists have been forced to give up instructive theories and adopt selective theories, so, too, must those concerned with basic writing give up their instructive theories and adopt instead a selective theory.

Krashen says that we can facilitate the selective processes of acquisition by encouraging reading, albeit with much-delayed results and no glory. Krashen's theory deals with the encouragement of acquisition in some detail. By making a distinction between acquisition—a matter about which teachers can do little in a tangibly productive sense—and learning—the area in which the teacher is essential—Krashen gives teachers a specific, central role in the mastery of language skills. The work of Kroll and Winterowd expands this role even further. However, it must be remembered that language mastery comes about principally through acquisition, and acquisition is something that can be facilitated but not taught. As Chomsky says, "keeping to the interaction of the whole system and an external signal, we see what appears to be an 'instructive process'; the system changes and the change is caused by the stimulus. . . . But processes which are 'instructive' at the system level, in this sense, 'imply selective mechanisms, through which products that are already present in the system prior to the arrival of the signal are selected and amplified'" (Chomsky, *Rules* 138).

The theory of writing acquisition proposed here is selective, rather than instructive in nature. It suggests that there are "selective mechanisms" and "products" in the system of basic writers which allow them to select and amplify the signal of academic written English as it comes to them in basic writing classes. The products in the system are a knowledge, albeit unconscious, of the inherent redundancies in language and an awareness of the important differences between spoken and written forms. The selective mechanisms, if the arguments presented here are correct, include acquisition and learning processes, ordered acquisition with errors partly due to inappropriate use of the monitor, as well as the use of comprehensible input and the affective filter. Chomsky notes that selective theories are superior to instructive theories, suggesting that the central hypothesis and corollaries discussed in the preceding chapters warrant detailed basic research.

Such research must address each claim of the theory separately. Support for all the corollaries will provide broad evidence for the central hypothesis that basic writers learn to write as others learn a second language because, for them, academic discourse is a distinct language. The first claims that warrant research attention are those that show the unique psycholinguistic features of written versus spoken forms. Although much has been written on the difference between speaking and writing, the similarities remain salient, and the question needs further study. In particular, new findings in discourse theory and in linguistic analysis, such as the work of Halliday and Hasan in *Cohesion in English* and Peter Binkert's *Generative Grammar without Transformations*, may provide stronger support for the distinction between spoken and written forms. Additional insights may come from new work on redundancy in language, even though redundancy is difficult to measure and test. The research reviewed here in chapters 2 and 3 already supports the position that formal written discourse is a unique language form.

Additional work with basic writers will be needed to support the other claims made here. Thus far, just a few detailed studies have been conducted, such as those by Bartholomae, Farr and Janda, and Lunsford. Additional studies will demonstrate the ways in which basic writers make use of both acquisition and learning, as claimed in the second corollary hypothesis. Case studies of basic writers, when available in sufficient numbers, will help teachers understand students' strategies so that they can teach more effectively. Similarly, case study research will show that basic writers, as predicted by the third corollary, acquire skill in academic discourse in an ordered fashion. The data may help us identify universal stages that writers move through as they work toward proficiency in writing. The description of the interlanguage stage presented here in chapter 4 and a first case study of this type in chapter 5 demonstrate the usefulness of the approach and the need for more data of this kind.

The data here and in other case studies support the fourth corollary in the theory of writing acquisition, which states that learned material works only as a monitor and helps to account for student errors. Here, again, discourse research along with further study of affective factors will yield additional evidence for this claim. The discussion here sends a clear message to the classroom: errors are signs of success rather than failure and students must err if they are to acquire and learn to write academic prose.

Teachers can also make use of the evidence on comprehensible input. The importance of comprehensible input, as stated in the fifth corollary, has been discussed here in several chapters—it derives from knowledge of the special features of writing, its redundancy, and the role of natural, meaningful language use as described in Krashen's monitor theory. The basic writing class must be moved away from drill and practice and toward meaningful language use for the students. Comprehensible input also comes importantly from reading, a necessary component of basic writing classes. Again, additional research can follow the impact of these changes in approach and test others to confirm the validity and use of comprehensible input.

Finally, little attention has been paid to the affective filter among basic writers, even though the few studies available support this sixth corollary, showing clearly that a lowered filter can make a significant difference to students' success in learning to write academic discourse. Some techniques advocated by textbook authors for all writers, like the conference-based approach of Dawe and Dornan, may be particularly useful with basic writers. This and other means of helping writers lower their affective filters should be tried and tested to uncover the most effective ways to enhance student learning.

Much work remains. The comprehensive theory of writing acquisition discussed in these pages, supported by some empirical evidence, marks a useful beginning. With a fully articulated theory, we can move to the research agenda specified above. Some of the hypotheses will necessarily be modified or changed as the data accumulate, but such changes will serve to move us closer to a "selective theory," identifying and clarifying how basic writers learn and what and how teachers can best teach. If basic writers acquire academic written language as others acquire a second language, then these efforts will allow basic writing teachers to serve the needs of their students most successfully.

Works Cited

Acton, William. "The Monitor Model, Monitoring and Language Acquisition Heuristics." Paper presented at TESOL Convention. Detroit, March 1981.

Adamson, Douglas. "Monitoring and the Monitor Model: Labov versus Krashen." Paper presented at Washington, D.C. Area TESOL. 1 Oct. 1982. ERIC ED 242 194.

Allen, Robert L. "Written English Is a 'Second Language.'" *Teaching High School Composition.* Ed. Gary Tate and Edward P. J. Corbett. New York: Oxford UP, 1970.

Andersen, Roger. "Introduction." *Pidginization and Creolization as Language Acquisition.* Ed. Roger Andersen. Rowley, MA: Newbury, 1983.

———. "The One to One Principle of Interlanguage Construction." *Language Learning* 34 (1984): 77–95.

Asher, James. "The Learning Strategy of the Total Physical Response: A Review." *Modern Language Journal* 50 (1966): 79–84.

Bartholomae, David. "The Study of Error." *College Composition and Communication* 31 (1980): 253–69.

Bereiter, Carl. "Development in Writing." *Cognitive Processes in Writing.* Ed. Lee W. Gregg and Erwin W. Steinberg. Hillsdale, NJ: Erlbaum, 1980.

Binkert, Peter J. *Generative Grammar without Transformations.* The Hague: Mouton, 1984.

Britton, James. "The Composing Processes and the Functions of Writing." *Research on Composing.* Ed. Charles R. Cooper and Lee Odell. Urbana, IL: NCTE, 1978.

Brown, H. Douglas. "The Consensus: Another View." *Foreign Language Annals* 17 (1984): 277–80.

————. *Principles of Language Learning and Teaching*. Englewood Cliffs, NJ: Prentice-Hall, 1980.

Brown, Roger. *A First Language*. Cambridge, MA: Harvard UP, 1973.

Cayer, Roger L., and Renee K. Sacks. "Oral and Written Discourse of Basic Writers: Similarities and Differences." *Research in the Teaching of English* 13 (1979): 121–28.

Chomsky, Noam. *Aspects of the Theory of Syntax*. Cambridge, MA: MIT Press, 1965.

————. *Rules and Representations*. New York: Columbia UP, 1980.

Collins, James L. "Dialogue and Monologue and the Unskilled Writer." *English Journal* 71 (April, 1982): 84–86.

Corder, S. Pit. "Idiosyncratic Dialects and Error Analysis." *New Frontiers in Second Language Learning*. Ed. John Schumann and Nancy Stenson. Rowley, MA: Newbury, 1974.

————. "The Significance of Learners' Errors." *International Review of Applied Linguistics* 5 (1967): 161–70.

Curtiss, Susan. *Genie: A Psycholinguistic Study of a Modern-Day "Wild Child."* New York: Academic P, 1977.

Dawe, Charles W., and Edward A. Dornan. *One to One: Resources for Conference-Centered Writing*. 2nd ed. Boston: Little, Brown, 1984.

de Beaugrande, Robert. *Text Production: Toward a Science of Composition*. Norwood, NJ: Ablex, 1984.

————. *Writing Step By Step*. New York: Harcourt, 1985.

deVilliers, Peter and Jill deVilliers. *Language Acquisition*. Cambridge, MA: Harvard UP, 1979.

Dicker, Susan. "Applying the Monitor Model to the Editing of Compositions." Paper presented at the TESOL Summer Meeting. New York, 24–26 Jul. 1981. ERIC ED 209 925.

Emig, Janet. "Writing as a Mode of Learning." *The Writing Teacher's Sourcebook*. Ed. Gary Tate and Edward P. J. Corbett. New York: Oxford UP, 1981.

Esau, Helmut, and Michael Keene. "A TESOL Model for Native Language Writing." *College English* 43 (1981): 694–710.

Evangelauf, Jean. "Enrollment in Remedial Courses Jumps at 63% of Colleges that Offer Them." *Chronicle of Higher Education*, 13 Feb. 1985, 3.

Falk, Julia S. "Language Acquisition and the Teaching and Learning of Writing." *College English* 41 (1979): 436–47.

Farr, Marcia, and MaryAnn Janda. "Basic Writing Students: Investigating Oral and Written Language." *Research in the Teaching of English* 19 (1985): 62–83.

Flower, Linda. *Problem-Solving Strategies for Writing*. New York: Harcourt, 1981.

⸺. "Writer-Based Prose: A Cognitive Basis for Problems in Writing." *The Writing Teacher's Sourcebook*. Ed. Gary Tate and Edward P. J. Corbett. New York: Oxford UP, 1981.

Gardner, Robert, and Wallace E. Lambert, *Attitudes and Motivation in Second Language Learning*. Rowley, MA: Newbury, 1972.

Goodman, Kenneth S., and Yetta Goodman. "Learning to Read is Natural." *Theory and Practice of Early Rèading*. Ed. Lauren Resnick and Phyllis Weaver. Hillsdale, NJ: Erlbaum, 1979.

Halliday, M. A. K. and Ruqaiya Hasan. *Cohesion in English*. London: Longman, 1976.

Hammerly, Hector. "The Two-Cone Model of Second Language Teaching/Learning: Some Further Thoughts." Paper presented at TESOL. Houston, 6–11 Mar. 1984. ERIC ED 243 335.

Hartwell, Patrick. "'Dialect Interference' in Writing: A Critical View." Paper presented at Conference on College Composition and Communication, Minneapolis, 5–7 Apr. 1979. ERIC ED 178 908.

Holm, John. "The Creole Core: Grammatical Interference in College Composition." Paper presented at TESOL. New York 8–13 Apr. 1985. ERIC ED 257 320.

Hsia, H. J. "Redundancy: Is It the Lost Key to Better Communication?" *A.V. Communication Review* 25 (1977): 63–85.

Krashen, Stephen. "Individual Variation in the Use of the Monitor." *Second Language Acquisition Research: Issues and Implications*. Ed. W. Ritchie. New York: Academic P, 1978.

⸺. "The Input Hypothesis." *Current Issues in Bilingual Education*. Ed. James Alatis. Washington: Georgetown UP, 1980.

⸺. "The Monitor Model for Adult Second Language Performance." *Readings on English as a Second Language*. Ed. Kenneth Croft. 2nd ed. Cambridge, MA: Winthrop, 1980.

⸺. "The Monitor Model for Second Language Acquisition." *Second Language Acquisition and Foreign Language Teaching*. Ed. Rosario Gingras. Washington: Center for Applied Linguistics, 1978.

————. "On the Acquisition of Planned Discourse: Written English as a Second Dialect." *Claremont Reading Conference 42d Yearbook.* Ed. Malcolm P. Douglas. Claremont, CA: Claremont Reading Conference Publication, 1978.

————. *Second Language Acquisition and Second Language Learning.* Oxford: Pergamon, 1981.

————. "Some Consequences of the Input Hypothesis." Paper presented at TESOL Convention, Detroit, Mar. 1981.

————. "Some Issues Relating to the Monitor Model." *On TESOL '77.* Ed. H. Douglas Brown. Washington: TESOL, 1977.

————. *Writing: Research, Theory and Applications.* Oxford: Pergamon, 1984.

Krashen, Stephen, Heidi Dulay, and Marina Burt. *Language Two.* New York: Oxford UP, 1982.

Krashen, Stephen, Tracy Terrell, Madeline Ehrman, and Martha Herzog. "A Theoretical Basis for Teaching the Receptive Skills." *Foreign Language Annals* 17 (1984): 261–75.

Kroll, Barbara. "Learning and Acquisition: Two Paths to Writing." ERIC ED 163 464.

Langer, Judith A., and Mark Nicolich. "Prior Knowledge and Its Effect on Comprehension." Paper presented at International Reading Association Annual Convention. St. Louis 5–9 May, 1980. ERIC ED 186 874.

Lunsford, Andrea. "The Content of Basic Writers' Essays." *College Composition and Communication* 31 (1980): 278–90.

McLaughlin, Barry. "The Monitor Model: Some Methodological Considerations." *Language Learning* 28 (1978): 309–32.

Meisel, Jurgen. "Strategies of Second Language Acquisition: More than One Kind of Simplification." *Pidginization and Creolization as Language Acquisition.* Ed. Roger Andersen. Rowley, MA: Newbury, 1983.

Munsell, Paul, and Tom Carr. "*Second Language Acquisition and Second Language Learning*: A Review." Unpublished ms., Michigan State U, 1981.

Neilson, Brooke. "Writing as a Second Language: Psycholinguistic Processes in Composition." Diss. U of California at San Diego, 1979.

Nystrand, Martin. "The Structure of Textual Space." *What Writers Know.* Ed. Martin Nystrand. New York: Academic P, 1982.

Olson, David. "From Utterance to Text: The Bias of Language in Speech and Writing." *Harvard Educational Review* 47 (1977): 257–81.

———. "The Languages of Instruction: The Literate Bias of Schooling." *Schooling and the Acquisition of Knowledge*. Ed. R. C. Anderson, R. J. Spiro and W. E. Montague. Hillsdale, NJ: Erlbaum, 1977.

Ong, Walter J. *Interfaces of the Word*. Ithaca, NY: Cornell UP, 1977.

———. "Literacy and Orality in Our Times." *The Writing Teacher's Sourcebook*. Ed. Gary Tate and Edward P. J. Corbett. New York: Oxford UP, 1981.

———. *Rhetoric, Romance and Technology: Studies in the Interaction of Expression and Culture*. Ithaca, NY: Cornell UP, 1971.

Perl, Sondra. "The Composing Process of Unskilled College Writers." *Research in the Teaching of English* 13 (1979): 317–36.

Pianko, Sharon. "A Description of the Composing Process of College Freshman Writers." *Research in the Teaching of English* 13 (1979): 5–22.

Pinker, Steven. *Language Learnability and Language Development*. Cambridge, MA: Harvard UP, 1984.

Rivers, Wilga. *Practical Guide to the Teaching of English as a Second or Foreign Language*. New York: Oxford UP, 1978.

Rizzo, Betty. *The Writers' Studio*. New York: Harper, 1978.

Schumann, John. *The Pidginization Process: A Model for Second Language Acquisition*. Rowley, MA: Newbury, 1978.

———. "Simplification, Transfer and Relexification as Aspects of Pidginization." Paper presented at the TESOL Convention. Detroit, Mar. 1981.

Schwartz, Helen J. *Interactive Writing*. New York: Holt, 1985.

Selinker, Larry. "The Current State of IL Studies: An Attempted Critical Summary." *Interlanguage*. Ed. Alan Davies, C. Criper, and A. P. R. Howatt. Edinburgh: Edinburgh UP, 1984. 332–43.

———. "Interlanguage." *International Review of Applied Linguistics* 10 (1972): 209–31. Reprinted in *New Frontiers in Second Language Learning*. Ed. John Schumann and Nancy Stenson. Rowley, MA: Newbury, 1974.

Selinker, Larry, and Dan Douglas. "Wrestling with 'Context' in Interlanguage Theory." *Applied Linguistics* 6 (1985): 190–204.

Shaughnessy, Mina. *Errors and Expectations: A Guide for the Teacher of Basic Writing*. New York: Oxford UP, 1977.

Smith, Frank. *Understanding Reading*. New York: Holt, 1978.

———. *Writing and the Writer*. New York: Holt, 1982.

Sridhar, S. N. "Contrastive Analysis, Error Analysis and Interlanguage." *Readings on English as a Second Language*. Ed. Kenneth Croft. 2nd ed. Cambridge, MA: Winthrop, 1980.

Winterowd, W. Ross. "From Classroom Practice into Psycholinguistic Theory." ERIC ED 184 127.

———. "The Grammar of Coherence." *The Writing Teacher's Sourcebook.*
Ed. Gary Tate and Edward P. J. Corbett. New York: Oxford UP, 1981.

Wode, Henning. *Learning a Second Language: An Integrated View of Language Acquisition.* Tubingen, West Germany: Gunter Narr, 1981.

Wrolstad, Merald. "A Manifesto for Visible Language." *Visible Language* 10
(1976): 5–40.

Alice Horning received a Ph.D. in English from Michigan State University in 1977 and taught at Wayne State University in Detroit, Michigan, before joining the Department of Rhetoric, Communications and Journalism at Oakland University in Rochester, Michigan. She is an associate professor of rhetoric and linguistics. In addition to articles on reading and writing, language learning, and psycholinguistics, she has published a reader for students of English as a second language and is presently doing research on the psycholinguistics of readability.